D0882446

WITHDRAWN

CONCERT SONG AS SEEN

Kinesthetic Aspects of Musical Interpretation

783.043
Sch58c

CONCERT SONG AS SEEN

Kinesthetic Aspects of Musical Interpretation

Sara K. Schneider

PENDRAGON PRESS
STUYVESANT, NY

For Richard Lally

Pendragon Press Musicological Series

Aesthetics in Music
Annotated Reference Tools in Music
Dance and Music
Festschrift Series
The Franz Liszt Studies Series
French Opera in the 17th and 18th Centuries
Harmonologia: Studies in Music Theory
The Historical Harpsichord
The Juilliard Performance Guides
Monographs in Musicology
Musical Life in 19th-Century France
The Complete Works of G. B. Pergolesi
Pergolesi Studies/Studi Pergolesiani
The Sociology of Music
Studies in Central and Eastern European Music
Studies in Czech Music
Thematic Catalogues Series

Library of Congress Cataloging-in-Publication Data

Schneider, Sara K.
    Concert song as seen: kinesthetic aspects of musical interpretation / Sara K. Schneider.
    p. cm.
    Includes bibliographical references (p.)
    ISBN 0-945193-49-1(c)   ISBN 0-945193-62-9(p)
    1. Singing—Interpretation (Phrasing, dynamics, etc.) 2. Movement, Aesthetics of. 3. Songs—History and criticism. 4. Concerts. I. Title.
MT892.S36 1994
783'.043—dc20
                                                        93-40766
                                                        CIP
                                                        MN

Copyright 1994 Sara K. Schneider

Contents

CAT Mar 27 9 5

3-21-95 mls 28.42

ALLEGHENY COLLEGE LIBRARY

INTRODUCTION

The Performance of Concert Song

In *The Interpretation of French Song,* Pierre Bernac writes about the sub-
stantive value of the performer's presence in co-creating and constituting
the musical art work. Perhaps to counter the absolute authority accorded
to the musical score, he lends force to his argument by garnering not only
the statement of another theorist, but also those of composers themselves, about the musical score's inadequacy to convey the living quality of
the music:

> The written text, however fully annotated, cannot contain the actual
> reality of the performance. Liszt, the very model of the composer-performer,
> said: "It would be an illusion to think that one can set down on paper the
> things that constitute the beauty of the performance." And Gustav Mahler
> went as far as to say that the essential elements of his music were not to be
> found in his scores.
>
> To treat the work with respect it is, therefore, necessary to go beyond
> the text. "Musical performance," says Gisele Brelet, "is not material realiza-
> tion, but rather the spiritual function that this realization exercises." All the
> interest of the performance lies in the fact that, to be faithful to the work
> he performs, the interpreter has to give his personal vision of it. Only the
> performer's *presence* can give *expression* to his rendering (Bernac 1970, 2–3).

Bernac's argument seems self-evident: Of course it is vital to consider the
performer's role in influencing the reception and perception of a musical
work. It would be difficult to disagree that a musical score is not an
equivalent of or substitute for the work as performed, but rather a limited,

visual representation of a lived, humanly subjective, processual, and primarily aural reality.

Yet despite the prevailing, rather facile, experiential acceptance of Bernac's argument, there remains considerable reserve among scholars of music in considering what individual interpreters actually do contribute to the musical art work. Twentieth-century histories of song, for example, are, almost without exception, histories of compositional techniques; they gloss over the considerable problem of how the historical practice of interpretation through performance (as opposed to scholarship) has influenced both the compositional process and audience perception of the song repertoire.

Where the question of interpretation is treated at all in the scholarly literature, the relevant terms—such as "performance practice" and "musical interpretation"—have historically referred to the ways in which performers have affected aural perception of the works involved. From this view, had only the recording technology existed in the eighteenth and nineteenth centuries, all the data required to analyze the nature and influence of this kind of "musical interpretation" would be available. However, neither the notational nor the strictly aural level of authority comprehends the full range of the impact the singer of concert song may have on an audience. As Chester Clayton Long has reasoned, writing has the advantage over speech that it can store and record it; audio recordings have the advantage over writing that they also preserve the sound of the communicating voice; film gains over both insofar as it records not only the lexical level of what is said and the vocal pattern of the speaker, but all the kinesthetic aspects of the performance (Long 1974, 195).

Consider the weighty responsibility borne by the recitalist: to create through his body alone all of the visual elements which on the opera stage are delegated to a team of designers. Bernac encapsulates the extent of the task:

> In the course of an event, [the concert singer] must be not one but twenty different characters, who, at times within the compass of just a few measures and without any visual aid, must succeed in creating an atmosphere, evoking an entire poetic world, suggesting a drama—that is more often than not an inner one—expressing one after another the most varied feelings: sadness and joy, quietness and passion, tenderness, irony, faith,

casualness, sensuousness, serenity, and so on. He must from moment to moment, from one work to the next, completely alter his inner attitude, his mind, and, in some mysterious way, even the timbre of his voice (Bernac 1970, 6).

The living presence of the performer of song makes a decided, but little-discussed, imprint on the audience's perception of the music. Whether conscious or spontaneous, the behavioral and kinesthetic choices the singer makes while interpreting demonstrate the degree of his subjective involvement and identification with the textual content of his song; express the singer's attitude toward his subject, his invisible interlocutors, and his audience; and allow us to draw conclusions about the world imaged in the song by that world the singer has, through these relationships, created visually for himself and the audience.

In recent years, the decidedly physical aspect of artistic creation has received greater attention from social scientists than from music theorists. Anthropologist John Blacking, for example, perceives all art-making as not only an eminently human occupation, but as one which grows directly out of the artist's nature as a material, physical being:

> The mind cannot be separated from the body . . . for it is in the areas of nonverbal communication, especially dancing and music, that we may observe mind at work through movements of bodies in space and time. . . .
>
> The essential function of the artistic process is to mediate between the impermanent and permanent in man to capture the force of feeling with forms that must always begin as extensions of the body. If the creation of a new aesthetic form may seem to be a product of conscious thought, I think that most creative artists will agree that it begins as an "explosion" of the body which produces apparently spontaneous results (Blacking 1977, 18–22).

Blacking here underscores the import of considering the physical nature of artistic creation. Artistic *interpretation* is certainly no less alive if it is true that the singer

> follows the composer's path in the opposite direction. The composer creates his music by giving it its living meaning, before writing it down, or while doing so. Whereas for the performer the work is presented as the very opposite of an improvisation: as a thing noted down, with fixed signs and of immutable form, the enigma and meaning of which are to be divined and spelled out afterwards (Fuertwangler paraphrased in Bernac 1970, 1–2).

The soundless behaviors and kinesthetic choices performers make in *all* musical genres and on all instruments, when viewed alongside their strictly musical choices, provide abundant material for study. Alone among Western classical musicians, however, the recital singer is interpreter of the relationship between the lexical and musical levels of the song and, free of external instrument, can move his entire body except as movement would affect the mouth and the tone-producing mechanism. This discussion focuses on the nature of extra-musical values in song interpretation as they affect and are affected by the singer.

Despite the physical capacity of the singer to engage in an unbridled array of physical actions while singing, the behavior-restricting conventions of the song recital are matched by few other artistic genres. At the root of these prohibitions is the strange fact that, perhaps like no other genre of singing, the classical song recital is fraught with an ambivalence about the proper scope of the singer's role. In the field there is widespread belief that, like an instrumentalist, the singer should not intrude his own personality upon the material: that he must merely let it shine purely and radiantly through him. Further, recitals reach, in number and seating capacity, a lilliputian audience in comparison with opera. A given program is usually performed only once per city. Due to the significant factor of audience size alone, the contemporary recital world precludes the formation of any cult of followers of the scope that opera stars tend to attract. Therefore, the relatively unknown recitalist employs a far more conservative, music-serving set of kinesthetic behaviors than does the opera singer either in his own medium or when singing recitals. It is the less self-referential behaviors of the career recitalist, rather than those of the opera singer in recital, which are of primary interest here.

* * * *

The performance genre of the solo concert—both vocal and instrumental—grew out of the concert societies in German-speaking countries, and out of the European pleasure gardens of the late eighteenth century. Prior to the formation of the concert societies, European noblemen and professional musicians had played side by side in court concerts: "The Court set the general tone, and in 1783 Reichardt, visiting Vienna, noted how the nobility practised music 'with passion' and how it was impossible to conceive of a more musical society" (Young 1965, 131). Two factors principally contributed to the growth of the public concert: A public that wanted to listen to music rather than to make it itself, and a municipal authority willing to support concerts (Raynor 1972, 314). Growth of the public concert was more rapid in rural areas than in the principal cities, because of the greater availability of opera, music at court, and *Hausmusik*.

The organization of the *Musikalische Gesellschaft* (Musical Society) in Germanized Warsaw in 1805 is cited as a crucial development in the rise of the public concert; it was a transitional marker between the amateur communal concerts and playing for others' enjoyment. Admission to the *Gesellschaft* was based on an audition or a test of musical scholarship. Members were amateur musicians who were required to play or sing for each other whenever called upon—or else lose their membership in the Society. The *Gesellschaft der Musikfreunde* (Society of Friends of Music) in Vienna was another significant early concert society, which in 1817 instituted a regular series of chamber concerts, called *Abendunterhaltungen* (evening entertainments), open only to society members and their guests, thus "turning chamber music for the first time into another form of public music" (Raynor 1972, 329).

The eighteenth- and nineteenth-century pleasure gardens, particularly in England, and the early nineteenth-century public garden concerts in Germany served as means of popularizing musical entertainment al fresco amid food and avid socialization. The criterion for musical programming was sensational box-office appeal; concerts included selections from oratorio, Italian opera, ballad opera, folksong, and adaptations of favorite instrumental tunes scored for chamber orchestra (Young 1965, 142).

In an astoundingly comprehensive compendium of thoughts on singing published between 1777 and 1927, Brent Jeffrey Monahan remarks the increasing attention to interpretation—both musical and physical—over the period:

> The 150-year span covered in this study witnessed a full swing of the pendulum from the dominance of the melodic line (e.g., the works of Mozart) to the dominance of the text line (e.g., the works of Wolf). In the eighteenth and much of the nineteenth centuries, writers basically confined

their discussion of interpretation to general considerations, to note-connection and to the most elementary of visual factors. . . .

The poetry of the *Sturm und Drang* and the Romantic eras allowed, moreover required a new subtlety from the interpretive powers of both composer and performer. Pure vocal powers no longer stood as the sole determinant of artful singing; therefore, in the late nineteenth and the twentieth centuries we find an increasing incidence of quotations discussing interpretation.

During this time, the development of the *Lied* form created a popular idiom, the solo recital. Thought had to be given concerning the order of presentation in the performance. Memorization came into fashion and freed the hands and arms for those wishing to use them for gesturing (Monahan 1978, 220).

In the late nineteenth century solo music began to tour, and opera stars found it profitable both professionally and financially to perform concerts, comprised mostly of arias, between opera engagements. As today, the accompanist maintained a low profile so as not to upstage the star. The heyday of the solo recital in America occurred in the 1940s and 1950s, with touring stars such as Lotte Lehmann, Jennie Tourel, Lily Pons, and Maria Jeritza, and the form crystallized into its present, rather orthodox format.

A typical solo song recital lasts between forty-five and sixty minutes and consists of between five and six groups of songs, perhaps twenty in all, selected by the singer himself and usually organized chronologically by composer or period or according to language. The creativity and thoughtfulness of the singer in planning a program is assuredly part of the artistry of the concert itself. Harry Plunket Greene urges singers to keep the overall shape and variety of the concert in mind when deciding on a program and lists among the requisite considerations variety of language; change of composer; chronological order; change of key; change of time; style of technique; change of tempo or pace; crescendo and diminuendo of emotion; atmosphere and mood; and classification of the song according to twelve types which he designates as atmospheric, dramatic, narrative, songs of characterization, songs of reminiscence, contemplative, songs of address or ode songs, bel canto, ghost songs, songs of question and answer, humorous and quasi-humorous, and folk-songs. Greene recommends that singers plot the progress of these qualities over a page in order to concentrate on variety in all the above modes (Greene 1979, 201–2, 223–24).

Most art songs are performed with piano accompaniment. (On rare occasions, songs will be performed with one or more other instruments, usually strings.) However, it is central to the *Lied* form—of which Franz Schubert, as the champion of balanced collaboration between pianist and singer, is considered the highest exponent and most influential composer—that the piano part be considered of equal importance to the voice; hence the term "accompaniment" is a controversial one. Despite the sometimes grudgingly acknowledged contribution of the pianist, the singer is always billed higher on the program, signals the pianist when he is ready to begin each song, and receives the overwhelming bulk of the critical attention (the pianist usually receives no more notice than "Mr. X assisted ably"). He is ostensibly the musical leader of the group, though it is widely maintained that the pianist is the more musically sophisticated, one of his tasks being to keep the singer in line on matters of musicianship.

In addition to signalling the beginnings of songs, the singer also leads in entering or exiting the stage. The musicians usually exit the stage between song groups in order to rest for a moment in private and to have a drink of water. The breaks between groups offer the beginning of each set as a fresh appeal to the audience's attention, like the cleansing of the palate between wine-tastings. Audiences are usually requested to withhold their applause until the end of each group so as not to break the mood established for the audience or the concentration of the singer within musically coherent sets. The holding of applause is evidence of the ethic that the music, rather than the singer, is the proper focus of attention in the recital. More practically, the acknowledgment of applause, especially so frequently as between every song, may become awkward for the singer within the intimate recital setting. Aksel Schiøtz warns against the danger of the singer's appearing to "overrate" himself, an evident danger when the applause is too frequent, though the audience instigates it (Schiøtz 1970, 176).

Transitions between songs are viewed as important parts of the singer's artistic design for the overall program. Bernac asserts that "In a

song cycle, the duration of the silences between the songs is very important and should not always be the same. This must be carefully planned
in advance" (Bernac 1970, 10). In terms of physical behavior, these transitions are often the most mesmerizing parts of the recital, since they provide the opportunity to observe a singer's slow relinquishing of one mood
and gradual adoption of the next. Indeed, one of the most engrossing
aspects of this transition is its timing, the span the singer deems necessary
to let go of the mood of one song and to enter into the mood of the
second. As Greene puts it, "The mood belongs to the singer, the atmosphere to the song. . . . It is not necessary to ticket either atmosphere or
mood with a name. The singer need only realise the meaning" (Greene
1979, 13–14).

In making transitions between songs, singers seem to draw their attention away from the audience and into themselves. To improve their
concentration, and perhaps also to mask these very open, vulnerable moments in which no music is supporting them, many singers turn toward
the pianist and return to face the audience apparently in the mood of the
next piece. Mezzo-soprano Christa Ludwig goes even further than this: In
a videotape of a 1973 Brahms Lieder recital at the Tel Aviv Museum, she
turns to face her accompanist not just during transitions between songs,
but during the postludes, and looks pointedly at him. Tenor and Juilliard
interpretation teacher Paul Sperry suggests that this technique might
have been thought to give attention to the piano part and to the pianist's
playing. Even if this is indeed the reasoning behind Ludwig's movement,
the habit also works quite expediently for the singer as a chance to diffuse
attention on herself; it becomes a means of making longer, less emotionally intense transitions between songs.

Singers may be instructed to use the postludes as a way to continue
the action of the song. In *The Art of the Song Recital*, Emmons and Sonntag instruct the singer to consider the following questions when determining how to perform silently the postlude of a song:

> What is the speaker's mental and physical condition at the end of the song?
> What happens after the text stops?
> What happens after the music stops? (Emmons and Sonntag 1979, 128)

And, although she assumes that the piano and singer express the same idea or mood, Lotte Lehmann pleads that "You sing what the piano expresses, you in your heart are singing the prelude, the interlude, the postlude . . ." (Lehmann 1985, 13). In a 1984 *Lieder* recital in Paris, Dietrich Fischer-Dieskau silently acted out during the postludes apparent thoughts and even events sharply in contrast with what had just been sung: thus, the culmination of the vocal line marked the end of a particular way of being and the decision (or necessity) to move on.

Since singers generally remain within a two-foot radius of the crook of the piano, physical aspects of interpretation are restricted to aspects of visual focus, facial expression, gesture, use of and relations among body parts, posture and stance, physical relationships to the accompanist and the audience, and movement within the limited space. Costume and gait are also relevant when examining visual aspects of meaning in the song recital. Because of the relatively limited use of translation of the body in space, the use of the eyes becomes especially important to indicate spatial relations between singer and imagined interlocutor or perceived object. John J. Allen describes the role of visual focus in oral interpretation as follows:

> One of the interpreter's most challenging responsibilities is to *project* the implied action of the text for the audience so that they experience his "seeing" it. Sometimes, of course, the action is not literal *activity*, but rather scenes or events which must be made vivid and clear. The fictive scene—whether simple description or complex human interaction—is never onstage with the performer. Instead, it is projected to the audience or into an imaginary realm in the vicinity of the audience (Allen 1984, 233).

These points of examination are similar for other studies of solo oral performance. In his dissertation on verbal and physical behaviors of the solo oral interpreter, for example, Allen identifies thirteen aspects of physical behavior as being of interest: Personal appearance; posture; muscle tonicity and readiness to respond ("vitality"); appearance of confidence and ease of execution; gestures of extremities, face, and eyes; movement (beyond gesture); use of a typescript; focus of delivery for speakers; performance conventions and framing techniques; preserving,

reducing, or eliminating ambiguity; introductions, transitions, and conclusions; reacting to feedback; and coping with performance blunders
(Allen 1984, 187–88). While a portion of Allen's purpose is admittedly a
prescriptive one, aimed at developing rules for a high level of performance
in oral interpretation, some of the variables he identifies have clear application to a descriptive analysis of solo physical performance.

Writers on song recital performance have their own prescriptive list
of the requirements of the advanced recitalist. Emmons and Sonntag list a
number of qualities and skills that the fine recitalist should possess: a well
trained and reasonably beautiful voice; advanced musicianship; an attractive and vital personality; the ability to project and communicate; the
ability to think and perform on many levels; the ability to go beyond what
can be taught; versatility of styles (for the American singer); musical and
literary insight and imagination; and good health and the determination
to keep it (1979, 21). On a more descriptive level, Paul Sperry assesses
the strengths of the recital singer, as distinguished from the singer of
opera, as the possession of a kind of flexibility in the sound of one's voice
and in one's dramatic ability, necessary in order to maintain the
audience's interest in a solo performer for an hour; a secure soft end in
the dynamic range; and the ability to value other aspects of one's art
equally with the sound of the voice, unusual in the financial climate
facing contemporary singers (Sperry interview 1988).

In this study, I outline the range of physical performance seen within
the song recital setting. My purpose is to begin to illustrate the array of
solutions singers have found—or in the case of performers deconstructing
the song tradition, *created*—to address the problem of a musically determined gesture. In order to approach musical interpretation from this
visual point of view, I am purposefully omitting all but the most cursory
comparison with what might be thought of an obvious choice, operatic
gesture, primarily because of the ideally interactive nature of physical performance in opera, the fact that in most cases in opera, movement is
staged for the singer by the opera director rather than created solely by
the performer as a direct, personal response to what he is singing.

In Chapter 1, I place recital singing within the history of solo performance since the baroque period, especially with reference to rhetorical
style and eighteenth-century acting technique, in order to demonstrate

the essentially eighteenth-century basis of the conventions of the form, despite its nineteenth-century development and many post-Stanislavski injunctions for acting style (as exemplified by the teaching at the Manhattan School of Music by Cynthia Hoffman and the pedagogical method of Emmons and Sonntag in *The Art of the Song Recital*).

From examining the historical nature of the recital's conventions, I view song performance in Chapter 2 as a process of learning acquisition whose physical style is reinforced by certain aspects of the pedagogical process in the university setting, the site where most recitals are now performed. Descriptions of the types of gestures and body movements characteristic of the singer in recital will find examples in the actual behaviors of students in song interpretation classes in the conservatory setting. Next, examination of the teaching style of three New York-based teachers will frame a discussion of how style is *learned* in an art form which has long privileged the *spontaneous* physical and emotive response to the material.

Chapter 3 examines song recital performance by comparison and contrast with closely related genres, particularly the performance of popular song in concert. In addition, analysis of the work of two contemporary performers, whose performance works deconstruct the song recital tradition, highlights the conventions of the form and the meaning of departures therefrom. The work of these two performers, John Kelly and Ira Siff, will also underlie discussion in Chapter 4 of the possibilities and meanings of a musically determined gesture.

CHAPTER I

Baroque Influences on Contemporary Style

Although *Lieder* singers did not tour until the late nineteenth century, the performance conventions of recital singing appear to be linked, rather than with nineteenth- or twentieth-century naturalism, with certain developments in acting, particular genres of solo performance, and aesthetic ideals, all rooted in the eighteenth century. During the baroque period, the Aristotelian doctrine of the *Affektenlehre* governed musical composition. Paul Henry Lang defines the *Affektenlehre* as a system of composition according to which "mental states, that is the feelings or 'affections' of man, [could] be represented in music by certain tonalities and meters as well as by distinct melodic, rhythmic, and harmonic turns and figures" (Winn 1981, 197). James Winn proclaims that the imitative convention took its cue from the Renaissance rhetorical tradition and its hunger to imitate through art certain emotional aspects of human nature.

Indeed, eighteenth-century writers on music, such as Quantz and Praetorius, expressed their belief that the object of the musical interpreter was essentially similar to that of the orator: to control the emotions, or "to move the heart and affections of the auditors [thus] permitting the song to accomplish its purpose" (Praetorius 1979, 169; see also Quantz in Dorian 1942, 139). Both rhetoricians and composers were concerned, however, that the scale of the imitation be suited to the occasion. Prefiguring Gilbert Austin's eighteenth-century injunction to the rhetorician, seventeenth-century composer John Dowland urged that the singer judge the nature of the occasion and suit the type and ardor of his music-making to that: "Let the singer discerne the difference of one holiday from another, lest on a slight holiday he either make too solemn service, or too slight on a great" (Dowland 1979, 160).

Partly due to this foundation of the *Affektenlehre* in rhetorical practice, Frederick Dorian argues that the *Affektenlehre* creed found its climax rather than its genesis in the eighteenth century. Yet Dorian also finds that ancient Greek, as well as some medieval and Renaissance composition, looked to a piece's key, time signature, tempo and verbal directives (e.g., *doloroso, maestoso*), as well as their shifts, as direct signs of the emotions to be imitated through the music (Dorian 1942, 138).

Despite the almost pan-historical attempts at emotional imitation in the arts, the humanistic basis of the swelling interest in interpretation itself found its true match in the philosophical milieu of the Renaissance:

> Interpretation is as old as the art of music itself. Yet, as the musical expression of personalized emotion and individual feelings, interpretation could not unfold its power as long as the medieval spirit recognized and controlled the arts only as servants of liturgy. Thus certain types of musical performance, essential today, originated as by-products of what the sixteenth century called *la découverte de l'homme*—the discovery of the human being. As Lang points out, the search for a new type of humanity appeared in literature before it was clearly perceptible in the other arts. However, the "scientific and critical spirit of humanism led art to methods which resulted in the discovery of linear perspective, anatomic studies, the construction of the human body according to mathematical measurements, and in music to the modern principles of harmony." Such departure from medievalism was bound to affect strongly the realm of musical interpretation: individualism appeared as the growing force in musical performance (Dorian 1942, 35).

To our contemporary surprise, interpretation was believed in the eighteenth century to originate not with the performer, but with the composer. As musical interpretation began to be viewed as the province of the individual, the composer was encouraged to undergo a role-playing process in order to produce, as if from the inside, a piece of music truly imitative of human emotion. Winn reports that Mattheson, in the eighteenth-century treatise on composition entitled *Vollkommene Capellmeister*, "even recommended that composers 'sink themselves' into various passions, taking on emotional roles in order to invent melodic expressions for them." Some poets of the period, such as Alexander Pope, also role-played with the rhetorical conventions of poetry and drew upon personal emotional experiences for their work (Winn 1981, 197).

If the composer represented actual human emotion in his work, it then became the interpreter's job to decode or reconstruct that emotion by working back through the music. Even in the seventeenth century, the singer of the newly monophonic music was supposed to identify with the speaking persona in a song in order to encourage his audience to feel empathy with him rather than merely to be entertained by his song. As Curt Sachs explains,

> In the seventeenth century, the singer was merged with the imaginary character to whom the poet's verses were ascribed. The singer had to identify himself with him whose joys and sorrows were depicted in the words. Hence music itself more or less abandoned vocal polyphony, and the monody, freed from the bonds of polyphony imposed on the voice parts, was not only inspired by the actual meanings of the words, but even by the speech cadence of the orator or actor. . . . Composers and singers were not satisfied to amuse or to delight their public; they wanted to move and allure it. This was a style to which the public was quite unaccustomed (in Dorian 1942, 49).

As the expression of personal emotion became a more prevalent criterion for composers and poets, the Romantic idea took hold that artists were people not only of rare talent but also of exceptional sensitivity. In fact, Winn perceives the *Affektenlehre* as a transitional movement between the classifying impulse of the Renaissance and the feeling impulse of the Romantics; "passionate self-expression" in interpretation rose with the death of mimetic notions of musical composition (Winn 1981, 259).

Just as he disilludes the common belief that the *Affektenlehre* principle was solely an eighteenth-century phenomenon, Dorian holds that Romanticism is not restricted to the nineteenth century, though he admits that as the century progressed, the appeals to the listener took a more emotional and less intellectual basis. In many periods, Dorian maintains, there was a

> subjective emphasis on the emotional, the fantastic, and the virtuoso element. . . . However, in the middle of the eighteenth century, a new musical style appeared, a style of highly emotional nature that embodied the seventeenth-century tendency toward an expressive music and the eighteenth-century interest in timbre (Dorian 1942, 217).

ALLEGHENY COLLEGE LIBRARY

Dorian finds it self-evident that the nineteenth century's waxing interest in a Romantic style of interpretation should find its greatest development in perhaps the most "intimate" of musical forms, the *Lied*, rather than in the more "spectacular" forms, such as the symphony.

Unlike the naturalistic acting style Stanislavski taught at the Moscow Art Theatre, which highlighted the vision of a director, emphasized interaction with other members of the acting company, and exercised ensemble values in rehearsal as well as in staging, eighteenth-century acting technique, like that of the modern recital, highlighted the individual performer. Even in scenes which represented intimate contact—for example, fighting or embracing—the actual physical contact was stylized rather than executed outright, thus always distinguishing among performers by keeping them at some distance from each other. In contrast with the sharp division between rules for acting in opera and in spoken drama today, the same rules governed both during the eighteenth century. In part, neoclassicists were struck by and wanted to restore the musical aspect of acting that they believed to exist in ancient tragedy.

During the eighteenth century, even onstage verbal communication was stylized. In the performance of a dialogue scene with two actors, the speaker always stood upstage of the listener; as the two interlocutors alternated speeches, they shifted positions on the stage so as perpetually to place the listener downstage of the speaker. Using this method, the speaking actor could at all times project his lines forward to the audience, fulfilling two aims at once: that of consistently remaining audible and that of flattering the audience that he always performed for their sake alone. An auxiliary benefit of this staging method was that the audience had uninterrupted access to the listener's reaction to the drama. Although he was not to turn his face upstage to face the speaker, the listener could turn his eyes to the side so as to appear to be listening intently. The speaker was free to gesture with his hands toward his partner and to twist or incline his torso slightly in his direction (Barnett 1976).

There is a strong resemblance between the physical performer-audience relationships in eighteenth-century acting and in the classical song recital. Although in the recital no one interacts with the singer as a co-dramatic character, the singer, often by his visual focus, "places" the characters whom he addresses in song somewhat to one side and over the heads of his audience, which gives them the same, slightly oblique, view of his eyes and face that the eighteenth-century audience had of the speaker in a given actor pair. In recital delivery, however, the torsion of the upper body and the possibility of gesturing slightly to the side with the hands does not follow the eighteenth-century model. Rather, the torso remains facing forward, the use of the hands remarkably symmetrical. One possible explanation for the greater symmetry of singers' movements around the vertical axis may be based on relative stage architecture. Audience seating for a conventional recital is usually much broader with respect to the width of the stage space to which the audience must attend than is the breadth of audience seating (in relation to stage size) in a proscenium theatre in which spoken dramas would be played. On the recital stage, a singer cannot afford to "lose" half his audience by making gestures to a side they cannot see.

A second hypothesis is that the eighteenth-century stage and the recital both favor, as their ideal of communication, that between singer and audience rather than that among stage characters. Unlike the naturalistic theatre, which emphasizes strong, realistic communication directly among actors, perceived by the audience from the other side of a "fourth wall," the eighteenth-century theatre stressed the relationship between individual actors and the audience; the torsion of eyes, hands, and upper body toward one's interlocutor thus became the only physical concessions to realism.

A third explanation might take into account the eighteenth-century views on the preferred positions of arms and legs in acting. During this period, it was deemed important to keep the body position open; where avoidable, legs and arms did not cross over the central body line. As in the baroque dancing and the courtly social stance of the period, the basic stance—probably developed largely because it was proven the easiest way for women to manage a costume of up to seventy-five pounds—was an approximately seventy-degree, turned-out third position, the heel of the front foot resting beside the instep of the back foot. When facing toward the right side of the stage, for example, the right foot was to be fixed forward, while the right hand was the one primarily used for gesturing. This technique also did much to keep the performer's torso directed as much as possible out toward the audience, which for the singer has the vital result of keeping the breath support as broad and unobstructed as possible.

In the eighteenth century, positions and movements of the eyes and eyebrows were also referred to as "gestures" and were largely codified. Roger Pickering detailed the expressions of the eyes in tragedy:

> In every rising Passion the Eye always makes the first Discovery; and, generally, in those more sudden and instantaneous. Pleasure and Joy lights them up to sparkling Brilliancey; Disappointment and Grief deadens them into Languor and Tears: —Astonishment and Fear keep them fix'd and open; Humility, Modesty, and Abashment under Conviction of Villainy, direct them to the Ground. Courage, Resentment, and Anger, make them roll, swell, and dart out, as it were, a kind of Fire; Tenderness and the softer Passions make them swim with a gentle, placid Mildness (Barnett 1979–1980, 5).

Gilbert Austin, expert on and codifier of eighteenth-century expressive techniques, listed the possibilities for positions of the eyes as "forwards, averted, downwards, upwards, around, or vacuity or vacancy" and presented examples of several commonly practiced ocular gestures of the period:

> The eyes are raised in prayer.
> They weep in sorrow.
> They burn in anger.
> They are downcast or averted in anger.
> They are cast on vacancy in thought.
> They are thrown in doubt and anxiety. (Austin 1966, 352, 475)

According to Austin, the first part of the body to react to strong emotion is the eyes, followed soon after by the rest of the face, the gestures, and by speech (Austin 1966, 381).

The authority which the eighteenth century vouchsafed to acting with the eyes remains key to twentieth-century texts on the performance of vocal music, though perhaps for a different reason. Here, ocular expression becomes an antidote for young singers who need to remove expressive stress from the critical sound-producing area around the mouth, lips, and cheeks. Compare with Pickering's outline Luisa Tettrazini's encouragement to the singer to concentrate facial expression around the eyes:

The singer's expression must concern itself chiefly with the play of emotion around the eyes, eyebrows and forehead. You have no idea how much expression you can get out of your eyebrows, for instance, until you study the question and learn by experiment that a complete emotional scale can be symbolized outwardly in the movements of the eyelids and eyebrows. . . .

Increasing anxiety is depicted by slanting the eyebrows obliquely in a downward line toward the nose.

Concentrated attention draws the eyebrows together over the bridge of the nose, while furtiveness widens the space again without elevating the eyebrows.

In the eyebrows alone you can depict mockery, every stage of anxiety or pain, astonishment, ecstasy, terror, suffering, fury and admiration, besides all the subtle tones in between (Caruso and Tettrazini 1975, 31–32).

For the earlier period, much of the fervid concentration on responding expressively with the eyes, rather than other parts of the body, came out of the physiognomic explorations which were popular, especially in Germany, in the eighteenth and nineteenth centuries. Physiognomists read moral and spiritual characteristics from the particular formations of external body parts, especially from the shapes and structure of the facial organs. Physiognomist Lavater quoted from *Daumer Dissertatio de Oculiloquio* on the supreme power of the eyes to reveal thought:

The eye appertains more to the soul than any other organ; seems affected by, and to participate in all its emotions; expresses sensations the most lively, passions the most tumultuous, feelings the most delightful, and sentiments the most delicate. It explains them in all their force, in all their purity, as they take birth, and transmits them by traits so rapid, as to infuse into other minds the fire, the activity, the very image with which themselves are inspired. The eye at once receives and reflects the intelligence of thought, and the warmth of sensibility; it is the sense of the mind, the tongue of understanding (Quoted in Austin 1966, 115–16).

Opposed to the efforts of the physiognomists were those interested in pathonomics, the relationship between dynamic changes in physical expressions and change in thought (Holmstrom 1967, 84).

It ought to come as no surprise that the eyes were championed so ardently during the eighteenth century as the gateway to the soul, since the visual arts were hailed by almost all the period's authors on acting style as the exemplar for the actor's self-instruction. While a great number of rules sprang up governing the portrayal of each passion through codified gestures, authors on acting technique issued rivalling statements to urge the actor to continually regulate the pictorial beauty of the stage picture.

Actors were to study the "postures and attitudes" of figures by contemporary painters, as well as those of classical sculpture. Audiences were pleased to be able to recognize in actors' performances particular postures from their favorite paintings. Frequently, actors even exited the stage holding an upper body posture which had been carefully studied and replicated. Eighteenth-century audiences were sensitive to the well-turned pose as much as to the well-declaimed phrase, and actors would repeat anything either posed or spoken that fetched a clamorous response. The result for eighteenth-century acting style, Dene Barnett reports, was an ability to adopt and relinquish certain postures quite at will. A director of opera and theatre as well as a scholar on eighteenth-century performance practice, Barnett has attempted to teach eighteenth-century techniques to his own performers:

> The widespread attitude of incorporating into one's role on stage the attitude and gestures of a selected painting or statue, provides us with a valuable device in teaching authentic eighteenth-century acting techniques to modern actors and singers, for they can be given photographs of expressive figures from painting or sculpture and made to imitate them exactly, with the aid of a mirror or another person, until they are able to take up the particular attitude, drop it, then take it up again, with ease and exactness. By such means the modern actor and singer soon acquire a keener eye for good posture and a certain valuable skill in posing (Barnett 1980–1981, 6).

Denis Diderot, in fact, wished to train his audience to view the stage as if it were a painting, to uphold an acute division between audience and stage (Holmstrom 1967, 38). It is vital here to distinguish how the separation between performers and spectators in Diderot's model differs from that proposed in Stanislavski's painting-like notion of the fourth wall. The first distinction regards the relative importance given to relationships among the performers as opposed to those between the performers and the spectators. In Stanislavski's theatre, the object was to create a convincing, magnetic world behind the footlights by focusing on the interrelationships and interdependencies of the characters, so as to draw the audience deeply into the depicted world. By contrast, Diderot was no more interested in naturalistic, character-based interactions among his performers than any other baroque writer, favoring instead the highly stylized, rather interactionally distant performance style which promoted embracing and fighting from a distance. Performers concentrated on physically projecting their character's emotions directly to the audience, not on relating those emotions to the onstage interpersonal situations that gave rise to them. Diderot consciously strove to create a two-dimensional stage world, in which audience members would have direct, cognitively based, aesthetically distant access to each of the characters, as opposed to the three-dimensional world of emotional identification favored by Stanislavski.

Another way to characterize the difference between eighteenth-century technique and early twentieth-century naturalism is to note that visual interest was created and concentrated at the level of the individual performing body in the baroque period, and at the level of the entire stage picture in naturalism. During the eighteenth century, contrast, opposition, and "stylish flexure" were all ways of expressing the means by which baroque actors rendered their stage positions painterly at a time when actors continually rearranged themselves over the stage space to preserve the symmetry of the stage mural as other actors entered. Actors always held their hands at different levels, turned their feet out, placing them so as to occupy different planes along the ground, and endeavored to maintain contrast of line between upper and lower arms, and between lower arm and wrist. According to a major treatise by Johannes Jelgerhuis, for the sake of painterly contrast within the hand (unless specific hand gestures necessitated another kind of placement), the index finger was only slightly curled, while each successive finger curved a bit more toward the wrist (Barnett 1977, 5). The oblique position of the eyes for listening, mentioned above, was similarly related to the desire for painterly contrast among body parts; the head, too, was rarely held straight on but usually at a slight angle to the shoulders.

Barnett has maintained that eighteenth-century acting was essentially rhetorical in style (Barnett 1980, 66). Neoclassical rhetoricians were required both to learn the appropriate gestures to accompany their oratorical exercises and to participate in the performance of tragedy and comedy (Massy-Westropp 1984, 127). Actors moved over the stage space as little as possible; as in oratory, gestures were used to punctuate, emphasize, or illustrate important words or concepts in the text. The intimacy of the connection between individual performers and the audience, as opposed to that shown to be possible *among* performers in the later naturalism, was essentially that between orator and audience. Austin was the principal teacher of and writer on gesture until the mid-nineteenth century, when Francois Delsarte established his own method. Austin's text, *Chironomia*, is a compendium of Western writings on gesture, particularly classical treatises, and was intended to benefit four groups of public speakers: the clergy, members of parliament, lawyers, and actors, though Austin believed that decorum demanded that the quality and effusion of gesture would be determined for each group differently. He explicitly likened the tragic actor to the orator:

> The dignity of the player's art consists in his ability to represent and sustain the higher and nobler passions and characters. For these reasons the tragic actor, who represents justly the manners and the feelings of a hero, has always been esteemed high in the rank of public speakers (Austin 1966, 242).

The resemblance of performance style in the classical song recital to those of oratory and of eighteenth-century spoken tragedy and opera acting are not the only comparisons to be made with the neoclassical performance style. Certain performance genres, either *silent* or using only *instrumental* music, popular during this period, also share many features in common with the behavioral and movement-oriented features of recital performance.

Discussion of these genres will help to highlight what may be inherent to solo and musical performance media—most strikingly, the use of relatively long-held or static gestures, consonant with the expansion of real time into musical time. Holmstrom wrote about the passion, during the period 1770 to 1815, for a new form of dramatic storytelling called the monodrama, "a literary text with musical interpolations which accentuate the emotional content of the text" (Holmstrom 1967, 96). Designed to combine music, declamation, and pantomime, monodrama was essentially a form conceived and created by Jean-Jacques Rousseau in 1763, when he wrote the one-act *Pygmalion* to prove that recitative could not be combined "harmoniously" with expressive music. As Holmstrom explained,

For Rousseau music was not an abstract form without expression. Since speech and music, as he says, cannot walk together he has tried to make one follow the other; every "phrase parlé" is prepared for by a "phrase musicale." When passion has reached such an intensity that the words no longer suffice, the declamation must be broken off and the violent emotion expressed pantomimically to the accompaniment of expressive music. Sound and gestures, Rousseau says, are man's original means of expression (Holmstrom 1967, 40).

Monodramas were generally quite lackluster, dealing for the most part with classical themes, and of lesser literary value than the spoken drama of the period. Holmstrom speculated that they appealed, however, to the "overstimulated palate of the day." At any rate, they were certainly popular for performers, since they provided the appealing opportunity for solo performance, and attracted singers whose voices were not large enough for opera. Though Rousseau invented the genre to prove a hypothesis regarding the proper relations of speech and music, the form endured as a means to experiment with the pantomimic expression of emotion, an area of particular interest in the late eighteenth century.

The authors of the early monodramas provided, in addition to music and text, directions for the performer's kinesthetic responses or behaviors. J. F. Goez provided five types of information about the physical aspects of performance in his monodrama *Leonardo and Blandine*: 1) analysis of the mental or emotional characteristics of each role, sometimes even without direct reference to the text; 2) treatment of voice quality, made always in reference to the actions of the breath; indications for 3) gestures and 4) facial expressions; and 5) suggestions of the underlying physiological changes—in, for example, the blood, breathing, or nerves—which would in turn influence the quality of the voice, facial expression, and gestures. Within Rousseau's script for *Pygmalion* can be found three directive columns: one each for the kind of music to be played, its duration, and the pantomimic action to be executed simultaneously (Holmstrom 1967, 40, 69).

The late eighteenth-century interest in matching pantomimic expression to emotion and in raising the interpretive performance of the material above the material itself is echoed in many late-nineteenth and early twentieth-century solo singers' approach to the business of staging recitals. Although it entertained much controversy about the propriety of physical performance elements, this period spawned a good number of singers more willing to experiment with recital staging conventions than has our own. Ursula Greville, interviewed by Frederick Martens along with nineteen other prima donnas and concert singers of the early twentieth century, perceived the physical aspect of song performance, even down to the choice of a "frock," as the means of making the song recital accessible to all:

> Most concert singers fail to draw the man in the street. They sing on a plane above him and do not make him feel at home with the music. And in many songs you have to make the impression you want, to fix it absolutely, *before* you begin to sing. Even before the opening measures of the piano introduction the audience must be gripped. . . . Try to establish the key note of each individual song before you begin to sing it (In Martens 1923, 27).

As Greville put it, if the singer pays attention to the visual aspects of the performance, at least she gives someone in her audience without much musical training something beautiful to look at. Another of Martens' interviewees, Emma Calvé (a highly touted Carmen), was criticized for her extensive use of gesture in singing performance. In defense she reasoned that gesture "is one of the means of effect, one of the ways of making the voice rouse emotion in the listener" (Martens 1923, 40).

Despite heavy criticism, Parisian singer Yvette Guilbert demanded that concert singing produce a kinesthetic realization to match the "thought" implied by its text, that singers become "plastically impregnated" by the song:

> I might mention here an objection which has been made so many times by critics. You hear them very often say: "The concert platform is not a stage. We want to hear singing but not to see acting."
>
> If such is the case, it would be sufficient to have singers show the purity, the power, the flexibility or the justness of their voices by singing the scale or performing other vocal acrobatics.
>
> To sing a song is to perform a vocal drama, where the vocal skill is not always of first importance. The interpreter has to create by his interpretative art the atmosphere; that means he has to create for the listener imaginary scenery, costumes, the different acting personages—in short he must materialize the text of the song (Guilbert 1918, 38–39).

For Guilbert, the relationship of primary interest in song was that between thought and living presence; ultimately, her performance style was bound up with the problem of how to realize one by the other. "Each song or each play," she asserted (quite controversially for her time), "is a pantomime without words" (1918, 80). Though other singers' testimony attempted to discredit Guilbert's approach by labelling her as more of a *diseuse* than a singer, her supremely visual way of expressing music is valuable to us in its drive to discover the source of specifically musical embodiment and gesture.

Within the eighteenth century's passion to discover gestural expression from emotion, gesture is often held to mediate between the cognitive, intellectual world of language and the emotion-packed realm of music. While Rousseau deemed speech inappropriate to express the stronger feelings, gesture takes flight after speech beds down, and is thus free to keep the performer's presence alive along with and in the music. In the French opera, as in the monodrama, singers generally alternated between "acting" during their recitatives, here using gesture, like the actors of spoken tragedy, according to the two principal rules of signification and pictorial beauty—and relinquishing such acting during their arias. Where Rousseau had deemed expressive speech and music incapable of coexisting, the French opera subjugated both text and behavior to the music.

In both the acting/singing texts of the eighteenth century and in later twentieth-century texts on singing one finds frequent exhortations to the performer to remain in character even when not producing speech or sound; through this direction, writers emphasized the importance of showing the physical life of the character through the body, at least as a substitute for sound. Eighteenth-century actors had continually to be reminded that one always listens to the other actors on stage and remains in character the entire time one is visible to the audience (not merely switching back into character when it is one's turn to speak). The corollary in contemporary singing texts is summed up by one of Harry Plunket Greene's three cardinal rules for singers, though phrased in significantly more musical terms: "Sing mentally through your rests" (Greene 1979, 92). Lotte Lehmann also urges singers to remember that "The song starts where the prelude starts and ends only when the postlude ends" (quoted in Schiøtz 1970, 23). Bernac explicitly treats the question of the performer's enduring physical presence even after having withdrawn his vocal "presence":

> In the vocal line of a song there are often silences, while the piano part goes its way. These silences, more or less long, may occur in the middle of a literary phrase, or of a musical idea; they should not be "dead" silences, and the singer with his "presence" must succeed in "making a bridge" between the two fragments of the phrase. The best way to achieve this linking of the musical and literary idea is to take a breath immediately and slowly at the end of the first fragment, and to hold it until one resumes again, instead of waiting until just before singing to take the breath. Thus the tension is held; it makes a great difference (Bernac 1970, 9).

The establishment of the performer's presence has only been discussed quite recently in significantly more natural, biological, or—as in the case of Schiøtz—breath-based terms than those of the more gestural baroque.

Another late eighteenth-century solo performance genre called the "attitude" contributed to the carriage of the century's spirited attempts to reform the living performer into a visual art work well into the solo performances of the early twentieth century. Unlike the spoken drama, the attitude was motivated by a sculptural rather than by a planar, portraitlike impulse. Practiced primarily by amateurs in a social setting, attitudes were the attempt to present (albeit sometimes within an actual portrait frame) a living representation of the "female figures of antiquity" (Holmstrom 1967, 238). The gestural systems and pedagogy of Austin and Delsarte, however indirectly, also led to a neoclassical urge to participate in what Genevieve Stebbins termed "artistic statue-posings"—imitations, in simple draped garb, of the poses and expressions of Greek statues (see Stebbins 1977).

In a sense, attitudes were the natural outgrowth of baroque acting theory: When actors were regularly urged to study and even to copy postures, "attitudes," and gestures from paintings to be used in their own characterizations in spoken drama and opera, a logical next step is the portrayal of painted figures for their own sake. The greater allure of the attitudes in sculpture also followed naturally once the actor's focus had been trained primarily on recreation through the body of visual art works, and once the relatively two-dimensional proscenium staging had given way to performance in drawing rooms, where the audience could have closer, and often three-dimensional, contact with the performers. One might think of the baroque painterly performing style within its proscenium setting as an attempt to make the performer into a viewed object, whereas the greater sculptural quality of attitudes and artistic statue-posings, as well as the later, more sculptural views of musical interpretation by such singers as Yvette Guilbert, revealed their performers' greater subjectivity—and deeper responsiveness to the musical material itself. Since the early twentieth century, solo performances in contemporary oral interpretation have resembled the later twentieth-century song recital in several structural respects: Both are presented in a stripped-down concert format, often in an academic setting, for a relatively élite audience which is attracted to the concert at least as much by the material (whether songs or literature) as by the performer; at the same time, both have a solid early history as essentially popular entertainments. In both styles, that performer is deemed best who illuminates the material most and who most gracefully delights in it without getting in its way.

The point of resemblance perhaps most pertinent to our present project is that both types of recitals have enjoyed bouts with a visually perceptible, even flamboyant theatricality which has raised significant controversy within the form and, in the case of the solo performance of literature, almost eradicated the genre within a professional setting. In his history of the one-person show in America, John Samuel Gentile tells how the new genre filled a need in a post-Civil War America for a popular, non-lecture entertainment for a newly literate population filled with a vehement anti-theatrical prejudice. The freshly burgeoning railroad system made touring for solo performers cost-effective. To succeed, however, this young form of entertainment had to dispense with the visual trappings of theatrical performance—the costumes, make-up, and scenery—as well as with any performers who might have given off a scent of the morally questionable world of the "legitimate" theatre.

The result on the first issue was a non-dialogic—that is, solo—form of delivery, on a simple platform stage which was not associated in the minds of the Victorian Protestant audience with the theatrical stage. In addition, rather than dressing in character, solo performers usually appeared, without make-up, in evening clothes—in a formal version of their apparent selves. Solo reading of literature was the ideal answer to the specialized entertainment needs of the Victorian era, and proved a profitable venue for authors of the day to read their own works. Many illustrious British writers supplemented their incomes by appearing on the American circuit as "monoactors," including, among others, Charles Dickens, Edgar Allan Poe, and Mark Twain (Gentile 1984).

Despite the similarity in program format, each of these three readers had a significantly individualized style which distinguished him from the others—not just as a writer, but as a performer. Dickens was the quintessential actor, luxuriating in the portrayal of his idiosyncratic characters. In contrast, more than a characterist, Poe was above all a wonderfully musical reader, and is reported to have "cantillated" his poetry for the audience. Twain remained scruffily informal, related rather than read his stories, and become known to his audience as a "personality performer" and humorist.

The popularity, profitability, and apparently unlimited latitude for individual stylistic variation along the solo performance circuit caused many amateurs to tout themselves as monologuists, readers, and elocutionists. Founded in 1874, the single, original Chautauqua Institution which sponsored readings (in addition to Bible study and healthful outdoor activities) led to the formation of a hundred Chautauqua affiliates across the country within a fifteen-year period.

As Gentile phrased it, "Ironically, elements within the one-person show actually helped cause its own fall from public favor" (1984, 43). The crazed abundance of available performers, many of whom were by this time crossing over from the legitimate theatre, plus a virtual plague in the 1890s of commercial schools sprouting up promising to teach elocutionary technique and tricks stolen from famous solo performers, contributed to the glutting of the field with performers of questionable quality, for an audience whose initially prohibitive theatrical prejudice had already been eroded by the genre's increasing theatricality. During the period between 1925 and 1950, the overcongested, undersubscribed performers' circuits tumbled, and elocution got a face lift within the newly formed academic department of "interpretation" as an enormous schism formed between its theory and practice. The aesthetic conflict within the field of solo readings, which greatly undermined its popularity and for a time its very continuation, concerned the degree of theatricality appropriate to this originally ascetic genre. As another austere art form, the song recital shares much of the shape, if not the exact dates, of the history that Gentile outlines over the last century for solo readings. Both began as popular entertainments, achieved their high points with famous performers presenting primarily nineteenth-century material, and quieted down to largely academic existences during the twentieth centuries.

The behavioral paths that the conservators of oral interpretation and vocal coaching have ordained in recent years within the university and conservatory, however, are at significant variance with each other. Oral interpretation automatically assumes written texts to contain in them implications for movement and for a specific spatial relationship between performer and audience. In Chester Clayton Long's terms, literature is heavily encoded in the body, and can be thought of as "behaved speech":

> A considerable number of aspects of a piece of literature can be fully understood only when the [performer] himself causes his behavior to assume a reasonable similarity to the behavior symbolized in the *spoken words* of the piece (Long 1974, vii).

Whereas oral interpretation pedagogue Long holds written language to contain seeds of performance behavior within it, teachers and performers of song repertoire increasingly during the twentieth century insist that the most minimal yet illustrative and "spontaneous" or "unconscious" gestures are the most appropriate to presentation in the recital format (see Greene 1979; Leyerle 1977; interview with Lucrezia Bori in Martens 1923:1–15; Schiøtz 1970). We can view this impulse toward the unrehearsed, "natural" physical form as the penetration of recital performance, already constrained by eighteenth-century aesthetics in its staging elements, by the concepts and preferences of the naturalistic techniques of spoken drama.

Whether a spontaneous approach to gesture in performance succeeds for the majority of young singers untrained in physical performance techniques is a prescriptive question. A more descriptive, theoretical project is to discover the types of gestures which can arise "spontaneously" or "unconsciously" in the performance setting, as well as the type of textual or musical source to which they refer. Just as eighteenth-century actors imitated figures from paintings as the basis for the expression of emotions, attitudinists referred without mediation to figures from the visual arts, and oral interpreters refer directly to the written linguistic text for their performance score, we seek to locate the inspiration for gesture in voice recitals. What is specifically musical about this gesture, peculiarly spontaneous about such movement?

From the discussion of rhetorical gesture above, especially as summarized by Austin, it is clear that eighteenth-century gesture underscored and punctuated the important points in speech: gesture and other forms of physical expression were thus used in order to enforce the message sent directly from speaker to listener. Austin emphasized how the attitude of the speaker is an essential element in impressing the importance of his message on the listener:

> The greatest principle of oratory is to impress the auditors with a belief that the speaker delivers his own genuine sentiments, and that he endeavours to persuade others only from the full conviction of his own mind. And of this sincerity, the natural indications are his earnestness of manner manifested by the tones of his voice, the expression of his countenance, and the force of his gestures: of these all men are judges, and in these expressions of feeling, all participate; and hence it is that enthusiasm and absurdity succeed with the ignorant, whilst even the wise and the temperate, are cold in their attention to the most excellent instructions, and the strongest reasonings otherwise delivered (Austin 1966, 86).

Austin's other injunction to the young orator is that he judge the extent and quantity of his gestural style in accordance with a sense of decorum and propriety based on his social station, the type of material he is reading, and the social context in which he reads. In order to perform the codified movements that Austin illustrates in the *Chironomia* at a level reflecting the speaker's understanding of the appropriate "decorum" for the given situation, while retaining that "genuineness" of approach to his own material, the orator must be fully immersed in the ways of merging verbal and physical oratory. Gesture must appear completely unstudied, spontaneous, and—though not entirely natural—unconsciously produced. As Anna Morgan, a Delsarte exegete, phrased it, "All gesture, to be natural, must be unconscious or seem to be so; the reason that studied gestures are often stiff, embarrassed, and self-conscious is that they have not been sufficiently studied" (Morgan 1889, 62–63).

In contemporary singers' advice on attitude to young singers, Austin finds his parallel in tenor Schiøtz, who has urged students not to distract from the music of the program with excessive physical behavior:

> In the performance of art songs the singer must realize that the program, not he, is the focal point. . . . To interpret actually means to explain. Thus, the singer should explain to his audience the contents of a poem by way of music. Singers are taught various means of presenting music to an audience. Facial expressions are essential; an immobile face will cancel out even the most beautiful voice. But only the singer's inner emotions should give rise to his facial expressions. Otherwise the audience will suspect that his expressions are not genuine . . . Gestures may be used, but they are dangerous; movements on the podium should be kept to a minimum and used only in very dramatic passages or when they spring spontaneously from the singer's emotions. More often than not they disturb and detract (Schiøtz 1970:19–20).

From cross-cultural research, contemporary anthropologist of gesture Paul Ekman drew three categories of gestures which he called emblems, body manipulators, and illustrators, which bear varyingly close relationships to linguistic communication. Emblems, for example, are gestures which substitute for words, possessing a specific, verbal meaning, such as waving to indicate greeting or departure, or motions which indicate the desire to eat. Of the three categories, emblems are the "most language-like of all face/body movement activities" and thus the most closely related to conscious activity (Ekman 1977, 45).

Gestures which least relate to verbal constructions and to conscious thought are the body manipulators, "movements in which one part of the body does something to another body part," or in which a prop is used "in other than an instrumental act; for example, playing with a pencil, twisting a book of matches, [or] using a paper clip to scratch an ear." While these gestures are in some cases signs of specific emotional states—for example, covering of the eyes may indicate guilt—usually an increasing frequency of body manipulators simply suggests an aggravation of anxiety or discomfort. Only in highly personal code systems would a body manipulator replace an overtly verbal message, for example, the tugging of an ear sent as a signal to a friend that it is time to bid farewell to a long-winded host at a cocktail party.

The final category of gestures Ekman designated as illustrators, "movements which are intimately tied to the content and/or flow of speech." Along with others working in the field of nonverbal communication, Ekman has identified eight types of illustrators in movement: batons, which accent a particular word; underliners, which emphasize longer streams of lexical material, up to several sentences in length; ideographs, which sketch the path or shape of thought; kinetographs, depicting bodily movements themselves; pictographs, drawing the shape of the referent in the air; rhythmics, illustrating the rhythm of an event; spatials, demonstrating a spatial relationship; and deictics, which point directly to the referent (Ekman 1977, 49). According to Ekman, illustrators are magnified as the speaker becomes more positively involved in what he is saying. They have a kind of flexibility of form, an uncodifiability which is unavailable to the more culturally patterned emblems. Illustrators have four principal functions in speech: "word search," the capturing or maintaining of attention while the speaker finds the desired word; self-priming or self-reminding; explaining through movement an idea difficult to put into words, and—as in Austin—helping to lend meaning through accentuation of what is said.

Since illustrators are the only gestures which explicitly accompany speech, they are most clearly applied to our inquiry into the quality and nature of gestures performed in the song recital. In light of contemporary writers' desire to promote only the spontaneous, unconscious gesture in song, it is interesting to note that the first three functions that Ekman delineates for illustrators—namely, word search, self-priming, and explaining through movement—are for most people and in most cases unconscious movements.

Ekman's categories were not designed after observation of artistic, but rather of natural, performances of gesture. In the case of the singer, who may be singing either as the incarnation of a particular character or as a narrator impersonating the character, the theorist must question whether it is the singer himself or one of the singer's characters who performs these gestures "unconsciously." Actors in the spoken theatre are accustomed to distinguishing between knowledge they as performers have about a character they might play and knowledge to which that character would be likely to have access about himself. Music theorist Edward Cone concludes that the singer acts sometimes as a narrator, sometimes as a dramatic character for whom the music represents the more global, often unconscious world of the character's thoughts and feelings:

> There are many occasions when the fact that a character subconsciously "hears" the accompaniment need not imply all its dramatic implications. Indeed, there are times when he obviously does not know everything that the instrumental persona knows. . . . In this regard, Wagner's orchestra has sometimes been compared to a "collective unconscious," in which each character participates to his knowledge and ability (Cone 1974, 36).

Cone compared the singer's transition between narrator and dramatic character to Joyce's "protean persona" in *Ulysses*, who "moves in and out of the thoughts of his characters; here narrative, dramatic, and esoteric techniques are combined; here conscious and subconscious persistently interpenetrate each other" (Cone 1974, 37).

François Delsarte's taxonomy of gesture provides a means of distinguishing multiple selves within a single character. The preeminent theorist of gesture during the nineteenth century whose teachings were infused by his fervent Christianity, Delsarte was no less a scholar on the workings of the speaking and singing voices and a classical singer who made a name for himself as an interpreter of Gluck (Shawn 1954, 19). Like the baroque acting theorists and the attitudinists before him, Delsarte directed his students to examine statues as examples of the principles of motion and expression that he taught. His theories, however, were misinterpreted by the distortions of overeager followers, and the late nineteenth and early twentieth centuries were filled with young dance students swathed in Grecian draperies posing as statues.

Delsarte's system was based not on a codified system of gesture like Austin's, in which expression was for the most part only contextually sensitive or variable, but rather on principles of movement which allowed for a variety of specific motions which could express similar emotions. As he cautioned potential zealots:

> It should be distinctly understood that gestures and attitudes, as hereafter represented, are given but one of the many forms allowable; therefore let no one think that if he has occasion to give any of them, he must restrict himself to the one form given in this volume. Nevertheless, in whatever form given—Meditation, for instance—the underlying principles hold good, that

is, the relative position of the head and body to each other (Warman 1892, 157).

Over fifty years before the James-Lange theory, Delsarte formed the conclusion that "Motion creates emotion" (Shawn 1954, 59). In the system he called "Applied Aesthetics" Delsarte divided movement into hierarchies of trinities, represented most generally by: "objective" motion, impelled by the person's "vital" or physical nature and reflecting sensation; "subjective" motion, relating to mental or intellectual responses and mirroring the patterns of consciousness; and emotive or emotional motions, paralleling the dominant sentiments experienced (Morgan 1889, 25ff.). Gross parts of the body he designated as representing in their motions primarily one of these three divisions. Within the trunk, for example, movements of the upper torso represented mental, of the heart region or middle torso emotive, and of the abdomen vital energies. Within each of these three divisions, three smaller divisions—mental, emotive, and vital—were drawn, then three further divisions, and so on.

Noteworthy in view of our interest in the relation between singing and bodily expression, Delsarte also divided the singing and speaking voices into the ever-present, but somehow persuasive, trinity: the mere sound of the voice represented the vital energy, tone or modulated sound was a function of emotive energy, and articulate speech arose out of mental forces. The ability to produce or resonate particular pitches was also assigned a triune status: predictably, chest voice was believed to come out of the vital nature and regions of the body, middle voice out of the emotive, and head voice from the mental (see Morgan 1889: Chapter 12— The Voice).

The Delsarte system of expression may shed light on the problem of determining what in classical song causes singers to respond and interpret it through movement. The very division of responding functions of the body into emotive, mental, and physical parts, as well as the determination of the dominant quality of the gesture based on the relative importance of these three elements, provides a basis for examining the gestures of the singing body as referring (respectively) quite roughly to: 1) the emotions experienced either lyrically, by an aspect of the singer himself which he attempts to express, or dramatically, by a character the singer impersonates; 2) the unconscious intellectual responses of the singer to the material, or to the mental responses of a narrator-persona the singer adopts to narrate a ballad or epic song; 3) the process of singing itself, given that within vocal instruction singers often learn particular physical gestures to help them visualize the placement of notes, the shape of phrases, or the action of the diaphragm, and that shadows of these gestures often remain unconscious yet visible elements in actual performance.

The sense of the lyric, dramatic, epic, and narrative modes are taken from Long, who posits a special affinity between the lyric mode and music because of their ability to "speak directly from the inner self to another inner self" (Long 1974, 124). If in the contemporary, gesturally conservative musical climate we accept Long's postulation, perhaps we can link the coincidence of the lyric and the musical with the preference in later twentieth-century treatises on singing for a more spontaneous, less overtly theatrical physical style: for in the lyric mode, one only "acts" as oneself.

Where oral interpretive techniques illuminate this study the most, perhaps, are in determining the particular spatial and temporal implications for the performer-audience relationship that are encoded in a song text Pamela Plax begins the project by asking of these various rhetorical modes such questions as:

> Where is the narrator?
> Where is the implied reader?
> Who is the implied reader?
> What does the implied reader receive?
> In what time frame is the implied reader?
> How is implied reader affected? (Plax 1976, 6)

When the issue of the visual aspects of aural communication is treated at this, the grossest level—that of performer and audience placement over the performance space—we can begin in more minute detail to read a song, at both musical and literary levels, for its implications for physical behavior. The temporal distortion which music then introduces to the expression of thought through words and movement becomes the barometer of emotional, mental, and physical rhythms, all of which adopt a temporally stylized—and at last, visible—shape in musically determined gesture.

Tenor Paul Sperry in concert

CHAPTER II

Modern Conservatory Training

One can readily see from the emphasis on opera studies in the Juilliard catalog that the school considers song interpretation a luxury art for singers, one for which singers and therefore the training schools themselves cannot afford to invest much time out of the infinitely more bankable opera. With noticeable chagrin, tenor and Juilliard song interpretation teacher Paul Sperry observed that contemporary singers are judged on the basis of quantity, on the size and tone qualities of the voice alone, rather than on the total interpretive and musicianship skills they may bring to the work, or on their ability to control expressive dynamic levels to a greater degree than is usually required of opera singers. It is, however, the balance and development of all of these skills, Sperry maintained, rather than the sheer size of the instrument itself, that determines the proficiency of the singer of art song as opposed to opera. Song interpretation classes tend to attract not only those singers with smaller voices, but also those with a particular love for the song literature, which makes more varied demands than does opera on their total artistry.

Based on observations at the three major New York music conservatories and at the Aspen Music Festival, I will describe in this chapter the nature of contemporary conservatory instruction and study. In addition, a number of theoretical issues related to song interpretation training and performance in the conservatory setting will be of concern to us here. First, how may we characterize the range of physical expressions which are easily discernible in—indeed, which are characteristic of—the beginning singer, and which are replaced with other behaviors as the singer achieves greater proficiency and experience in the recital setting? Second, what behaviors are created and reinforced by the structure of the learning process itself? Finally, can we relate the differential demands of the instructional setting and those of the professional recital world to the differences in performance behavior perceptible in student and professional recitalists?

In general, the gestures and other physical behaviors exhibited by the beginning singer readily distinguish him from the professional singer on the basis of their locus of reference. Specifically, the physical expressions of the beginning singer tend to reveal more about himself in the process of the *work* of singing a particular song than they disclose his ideas for enactment within or upon the fictional *world* of the song: who the character represented is and how he characteristically behaves; what his relationship is with the people to whom he believes he is singing; and what the words mean to him and why he is saying them in this peculiar musical way—or, in an alternative, more detached sense, how the singer shows his attitude toward the character, his social world, and the way he chooses to perceive that world and to express himself.

I shall only remark for now that my general distinction between "work" and "world" is not completely cut and dried; the two behavioral categories may interpenetrate. For one, there may be times when "work habits" become inadvertently expressive of character. In addition, the habit of "marking" the directions of a voice teacher, voice coach, song interpretation teacher, or master teacher may furnish an instance of the cross-fertilization between work and world, where marking is taken to mean either showing the instructor through minuscule body movements one's understanding of instructions or modifications, or using such body movement as an instrumental means of memorizing the appropriate bodily response which go with the performance of the requested actions.

Below I will discuss and provide examples of the varieties of work and world behaviors—the former in some detail, the latter only briefly, because I will deal with them in the work of specific performers in chapter 3. All examples should be considered in terms of the singer's or singing persona's relationship to the "real" demands of, or his responses to, the performance situation or to the fictive world implicit in or superimposed by the singer onto the song. This criterion of relationship deals critically with how the singer perceives his performance material and with how he situates himself within the performance setting. Unlike the gestural system of Ekman, for example, which concentrates at the micro-level on the relationship between the shape and type of gesture and what is being said, this approach allows for a special reflexivity; it permits the examination of gesture related to the act of gesturing itself, an essential provision when one takes account not only of the extreme self-consciousness of singers in solo performance, but of the musical world's ambivalence about the very use of gesture in recital as opposed to staged dramatic forms which permit and demand movement over the stage space.

It should be clear from the outset that in most cases, work gestures show the singer acting against, or getting in the way of, the expressive value of a song rather acting in concert with it. John J. Allen termed these movements which reveal the performer's "nonverbal interference with the performance act" "kinesic stammering" or "kinesic static" (Allen 1984, 224). They are probably found at their most ample and emotionally strenuous in scenically stripped-down solo performance forms which leave the bulk of gestural choices open to the performer, such as rhetorical delivery, oral interpretation of literature, stand-up comedy, and concert singing. This most elementary level of gesture and physical behavior demonstrates the singer's relationship to the mere act of performance.

Termed by others "autistic gestures" or in colloquial terms "fidgeting," Allen also named these gestures "adaptors": They are "movements of the hands, lips, fingers, eyes, and so forth, that are used to manage or vent emotion. These may be generalized or context-bound, and sometimes they are compulsive, i.e., deliberately engaged in" (Allen 1984, 210). Examples in the stiffly armored performing positions of many nervous singers are the scarcely perceptible toying with the hem of one's sport jacket or the continual smoothing over of one's skirt. Often, as Allen remarked, these gestures can represent the singer's ongoing commentary or editorialization on his own performance. Primitive protective gestures also play an enormous—even a humorous—part in the delineation of the singer's relationship to the physical and emotional fact of performing. I have often seen singers in an audition stand with hands clasped closely over their abdomens or pelvises, as if representing in a concrete fashion their sensation of being artistically "naked" to the audience's judgment.

While Allen remarked that autistic gestures may be performed quite deliberately, it should be noted that when adaptors are seen in the context of a stage performance, as opposed to during everyday speech, just the opposite may be true. It is vital to mention that so-called autistic singing gestures often appear to spectators—and subjectively feel to student singers—disturbingly involuntary or out of control. In a song interpretation class conducted by Antonia Lavane at the Mannes College of Music, one student singer spoke of the sensation that her arms were rising up to her waist level in spite of her conscious desire to remain still. Other students, too, speak especially of their arms as having a kind of volition of their own which is separate from what the singer himself wills as his physical interpretation of the song.

The conflict—to gesture or not to gesture—seems in part to be due to the infamous diversity of views among teachers, coaches, and audience members about the degree and kinds of physical behavior which are appropriate to or pleasing in song recital performance, as well as to the structure of teaching song interpretation in the conservatory setting. Disconcertingly, singers encounter vastly different justifications for, or criticisms of, the same physical behaviors from their voice teachers, coaches, song interpretation teachers, and opera directors, who, for example, may all coach singers to keep their shoulders low and relaxed, even during an excited, tense piece because, respectively: 1) hunching the shoulders creates tension in the throat, and is therefore unhealthy for the voice; 2) the extreme position of the shoulders distracts visually from the musical line and structure of the song; 3) the cramping of the shoulders makes the singer appear less emotionally accessible, and therefore less attractive to the audience; and 4) the character in question would be more likely to express her frenzy with darting, uncontrolled movements. I have purposely chosen an instance in which each of those commenting on the student's behavior makes the same judgment to try to eliminate the body tension or gesture (depending on how you look at it), in order to demonstrate that even the array of possible reasons for making a single judgment may present the student with a bewildering range of problem-solving strategies, any one of which may come to his mind when deciding in rehearsal or performance whether to keep or eliminate a particular physical expression. The different reasonings for a single judgment may contribute to singers' sensation of involuntariness in their movement, which they then attempt to edit and consciously to control.

Other types of involuntary gestures are what music-theater teacher, opera director, and author Wesley Balk would call "entanglements": particular, persisting associations between specific vocal mannerisms and movement patterns which are unintended by the singer (Balk 1985). Entanglements represent the relationship between the performer and the singing process itself. Many sopranos, for example, raise their eyebrows with successively higher pitches and hold them along with sustained notes. Singers for whom the type of breathing necessary for singing consumes much of their physical and mental energy often "flap" their arms forward slightly from the elbows with the swelling intake of breath, like a bellows. In addition to indicating movement patterns, Balk's definition of entanglements also encompasses cases in which parts of the body are held in order to sing or even to create particular vocal effects.

Because vocal production is often conceptualized as a process of engaging the involuntary musculature of the throat by means of mental imagery, many voice teachers speak of the singing process as one in which the singer simply allows a natural physical response to become disclosed. Under this conception, the student singer is to uncover characteristic physical tensions, rather than to consciously superimpose onto the body a wholly foreign set of physical behaviors as, for example, in ballet instruction. Thus, much voice teaching concerns itself with unlocking the various tensions in the diaphragm, chest, back, neck, throat, and face which "prevent" the appropriate vocal actions from occurring. Few voice teachers go beyond removing the tensions which prevent the proper tone from emerging, toward, that is, instructing their students in expressive or interpretive rather than in simply freeing physical techniques.

Many entanglements may be thought of as vocal "indicators," self-reminding gestures which are rehearsed in voice lessons and practiced as a means of imaging the inner motion of the involuntary musculature responsible for certain vocal actions and effects. Such indicators parallel the motion (often only imagined) of the diaphragm in breathing or the placing of the sound against the vocal resonators, as, for example, the horizontal cutting in of the hand rhythmically against the diaphragm region or the soaring and spiraling of a hand over the head as a tone is placed within the head voice of a tenor or soprano. Certain gestures combine the features of the adaptor and those of the entanglement, as when singers attempt visibly to rid themselves of tension by twisting the head slightly or by flexing the fingers of one hand. Alternatively, singers occasionally signal show-off notes with grand, spread arms.

A factor which may influence the production both of autistic gestures and of entanglements is the performer's desired relationship with his audience. The way in which the singer structures the interaction with his audience projects a particular performing persona, especially in the transitions between songs, in the introduction to the concert, and in the acknowledgment of applause. Perhaps inordinately self-conscious about the power their movement has to influence the audience's perception of them, many singers move in an excessively and studiously "graceful" way, or mimic in recital, without particular expressive relation to the content of their song, the positions and motions of ballet. They stand, for example, in first position, step forward from the hip rather than the knees, or make tiny port de bras with their forearms or wrists.

The authors of *The Art of the Song Recital* count among the requirements of a recitalist "an attractive and vital personality" (Emmons and Sonntag 1979, 21). When coaching a singer in class performing Charles Ives' cowboy song "Charlie Rutledge," Sperry stressed that, although the singer's diction should be modified somewhat to reflect the Western origin of the character of the song, the characterization must not be so extreme—that is, perhaps, out of keeping with the formal atmosphere of the song recital—that the singer no longer appears attractive to the audience. The singer thus toes a delicate line between making such a character believable and maintaining an accessible, appealing stage persona overall.

Several of these elements are closely interconnected: The fixed smile of the singer who wishes desperately to be accepted by her audience may also be seen as an entanglement between the tense, held musculature of her mouth and the business of making sound. Many teachers respond to the movement entanglements of their students by teaching them to freeze the offending part of the body, to make it lie (only apparently) passive against the process of singing—hence the tight association among performer-audience relationship, presented self-image, and unobstructed performance style.

Indicating may take place not only at the level of vocal effort, but at the level of the musical score and its demands on the performer. Almost without fail when learning a piece (or when *performing* learning a piece in front of their classmates), singers indicate musical structure with physical mannerisms. They shift one foot along the ground at the beginning of sung phrases (as they begin to expend a new breath) or plié to help them keep on top of dotted rhythms. They may move their heads jauntily from side to side in time with syncopated rhythms, or jangle them regularly with the runs of baroque music. Above all, some singers conduct themselves visibly as they sing, with cyclic motions of their lower arms, marking hard the downbeats in difficult modern music as if demonstrating the varying effortfulness of the pedal cycle when bicycling uphill.

In indicating musical structure with physical mannerisms, singers may be doing several things, among them mirroring the prescriptive conducting motions or the responsive kinesthetic movements of their teachers and colleagues when listening in class to the performance of the work. Through gestures that somehow replicate musical structures, singers may also reproduce in performance the gestures they use prescriptively or mnemonically in their practice sessions in order to bridge the gap between how they conceive of a piece musically and their physical ability to execute their conception.

It may be more distracting for a spectator to watch a singer perform an emotional song while indicating physically its musical structure than if he displayed extensive physical entanglements among his body, face, and the physical mechanisms involved in singing such an impassioned song. At the level of the music, there is a split between the knowledge the singing persona is thought to have access to about his musicalized world and his ability to communicate through it without being aware of its stylization. As I remarked in chapter 1, Edward Cone drew a distinction among three "personas" of a finished song, which he designated as the vocal persona, the instrumental persona, and the complete musical persona (Cone 1974, 17). What the vocal persona, or the character who is singing, "knows" about the world of the song may be quite separate from the knowledge the instrumental (usually pianistic) persona has about the world of the song. The accompaniment

> may . . . refer to the environment of the character (as in "Erlkoenig" or "Der Leiermann"), or to his actions, gestures, and physical condition. It is thus evidently "conscious" of the character—as a narrative persona must be. It can present either the character's point of view or its own, or a combination of the two. . . .
>
> The accompaniment does something else as well. By placing the voice in a larger formal context—a more connected melodic line, a clearer harmonic progression, a more complex rhythmic design—it symbolically suggests both the impingement of the outer world on the individual represented by the vocal persona, and the subconscious reaction of the individual to this impingement. That is why in "Erlkoenig" and "Der Leiermann" we hear not the actual sounds of hooves and hurdy-gurdy, but a transformation of those sounds—consciously [the protagonist] neither knows that he is singing nor hears the accompaniment, but his subconscious both knows and hears (Cone 1974, 35).

The complete musical persona represents the composer's own total level of awareness of the world of the song, as well as the ideal level of identification and participation for the audience, despite the more humanly accessible quality of the voice. According to Cone, the singer's job is to represent a character who is often quite unconscious of the technical work of performing song. Cone presented poetry as an example to reflect on the "unnaturalness" of stylized expression for any, even an elevated, character:

> As in song, such formalization must take place outside the conscious thought of the characters: We cannot suppose that Hamlet realizes he is speaking English blank verse instead of Danish prose. Hamlet's use of English is a necessary convention, without which Shakespeare would have been unable to write the play, or many of us to understand it; but the elevated verse he employs is an expressive medium that permits the voicing of emotions and thoughts usually unverbalized at the subconscious level of ordinary speech (Cone 1974, 34–35).

Perhaps because the singer exhibits a greater musical awareness of his world than the vocal persona, while singing itself remains an eminently human activity, it is easier to ignore the entanglements of singing than to fail to note indications of the song's musical structure within song performance.

To review, singers may exhibit a wide range of behaviors, grouped here as "work" expressions, which display singers' own efforts in performing a song and which for the most part are separate from interpretive ideas as applied to the material. These behaviors have been described according to a kind of spoke-like system which places the singer at the center of the wheel and branches out to the singer's multitude of relationships: with himself, his self-image, and his satisfaction with his performance; with the audience; with the act of making gestures at all; with the technical demands of the singing process; and with the technical features of the musical work he is performing.

In brief, gestures of the "world" type can disclose two basic attitudes. First, they may reveal the attitudes of the singing persona toward the fictive situation in which he finds himself expressing or communicating his thoughts. This kind of expression shares in the aspects noted above in the singer's relationship to the performance situation: his relationship with himself, his self-image, and his satisfaction with his performance. For example, the character may react physically to show how successfully he feels he is performing a serenade, which would also represent a reaction to the implied audience to whom he sings.

The second type of attitude which "world" behaviors may reveal revert back to the attitudes of the singer, as an interpretive artist, toward the *content* of the song—its poetry, themes, style of expression, rhythm, melodic line, etc.—rather than to the effort and stresses of singing, making music, or performing. In chapter 3, I will examine world behaviors in greater detail when dealing with two specific cases: performance artist John Kelly's extreme adoption of physical and musical attitudes toward his song material, and recital parodist Ira Siff's overlapping of singer and vocal persona attitudes, since he has created a character or singing persona who is herself a singer.

Here, I will discuss the pedagogical styles and their effects on learning of three New York-based song interpretation teachers, all of them recitalists who have had international careers: Antonia Lavane of the Mannes College of Music, Cynthia Hoffman of the Manhattan School of Music, and Paul Sperry of the Juilliard School.

As young undergraduates, students in Antonia Lavane's song interpretation class at the Mannes College of Music are the youngest group in
New York conservatory song classes. Perhaps because at the time of my
observation her students were preparing material for an upcoming class
recital, Lavane placed special emphasis on coping with stage fright, dealing with the singer's relationship with the performance situation and with
the audience. At length, she shared techniques she gleaned from her experience as a *Lieder* singer to help her students deal with the fragility of
the performance constructively, to help them overcome their sensations
of nakedness and ungovernability, and to establish an appropriately intimate relationship with the audience. Lavane suggested that her students
imagine, as they began their set of three songs each for the group recital,
that they had already been singing before this audience for some time—
that this performance was the middle rather than the beginning of a
longer event.

In common with the other teachers I observed, Lavane never gave
her students precise suggestions for a gesture to be used for a particular
moment within a song. Her physical suggestions lay more within the
realm of helping her students identify the ways in which they could make
the performance situation as comfortable for themselves and as intimate
for their audience—in short, as like the original parlor *Hausmusik* performance style—as possible. Therefore, rather than emphasizing specific interpretive techniques and choices of the body, Lavane dealt primarily
with the general scale and range of gestures as they affected the way in
which the audience would judge how accessible and comfortable the
singer was. For example, Lavane frequently made a distinction between
the size of gesture appropriate to the opera stage and that which seems fit-
ting to the recitalist's platform.

As she demonstrated the difference between the two, it seemed that
the salient distinctions between operatic and recital gesture are their size
and where they take place with respect to the singer's body. For Lavane,
recital-appropriate gestures take place in the very near kinesphere;
operatic gestures can penetrate the middle-reach space. While this distinction seems to be based on Lavane's opinion that large-scale behaviors
are off-putting to an audience when addressed directly to them (whereas
they would not be when addressed to another onstage character), there is

some interpretive decision-making in Lavane's point as well: The subtle feelings and intimate objects which form the principal material for art songs are more appropriately expressed with minute physical behaviors, partly because the audience should see the character's strain to discuss these personal matters in public at all.

It is noteworthy for our study of recital performance style and its transmission that the smaller the scale of possible movement of a body part, the more attention Lavane devoted to discussing its expressive qualities for a particular song, beyond making a judgment of whether it was [inappropriate] to the recital setting per se. Lavane avowed that the most important expressive equipment a recitalist possesses, after her voice, are her face and eyes. Next, the singer's most important source of expression is her breath, which should be considered a dramatic, communicative instrument rather than as a strictly musical one.

The student's growing consciousness of the effects of visual focus, and of the importance of making conscious choices about such focus, played a particularly strong role in Lavane's teaching. The eyes perform three vital, closely related functions bound up with the nature of recital singing. First, as they cause the beginning singer to focus on the audience by "getting interested in them," they can ameliorate the nervous singer's stage fright. The mere retraining of the eyes can thus relieve stress on the singer by placing the spotlight on the audience rather than on himself and his own performance.

Second, the eyes serve as a critical element in the process of communication by ensuring that the singer's "message" reaches the audience directly. This broadening of the singer's world places the emphasis on sharing what one feels in singing rather than on fully and privately experiencing it (as in some naturalistic stage acting), and places the burden of responsibility on the singer for ensuring that the audience understands the song, rather than depending on the audience to empathize with the singer's privately experienced world. (Lavane considers the recital setting a place for dialogue between audience and performers.) Her emphasis on communication between performer and audience during the song recital is also bound up with her suggestion that when one really wishes to communicate in performance, one focuses on the intention to say something specific—that is, the singer trains her attention on what she wants to say—rather than obsessing self-consciously on how she is going to say it, on the utterance's technical demands.

The final purpose of monitoring visual focus is to ensure that the singer remains accessible to the audience, since Lavane maintains that the concert singer will only be able to communicate successfully through the music if the audience perceives her as accessible. In order to maintain a *Hausmusik*-like intimacy with the audience, the performer's eyes should usually be focused within the realm of the immediate audience, to minimize the distance between the performer and the audience. Only when discussing huge subjects "like God, Heaven, Hell, Fate, etc." should the eyes be focused into remote space, out of the realm of the immediate audience.

Even more subtle than the use of the eyes in concert performance of song is the singer's use of her breath for dramatic ends. Lavane demonstrated how we often hold a child's attention by a sharp intake of breath before speaking to him, saying, "Come here, I have something to tell you." The opening and closing of the torso with the inhale and exhale of the breath helps, she asserts, to make clear what is happening in a given song by showing the relationship of the singer or character to what she sees (e.g., approaching danger). The breath can also be used dramatically to show how the singer feels about expressing the content of the song (quite often, the difficulty of saying such personal things as one utters in art songs).

In contrast even to Lavane's subtle treatment of physical behavior in recital stands Cynthia Hoffman's more dramatic, less situation-based approach to recital performance training. Vocal Performance instructor at the Manhattan School of Music, Hoffman trained her singers in improvisatory, largely naturalistic dramatic techniques which develop and deepen the singer's relationship to (for her, this usually means empathy with) what he sings. Singers assigned ages to the characters who sing the song. They developed points of empathy between themselves and the vocal personae of their songs. They paraphrased in their own words the poetry of their songs and, in response to prompting questions from Hoffman, improvised language around the situations represented in them. Any discussion of physical behavior for its own sake was notably absent and the result of Hoffman's dramatistic approach on her students' physical behavior remarkably indirect, even where Hoffman herself used physical coaching techniques to draw a response from the student.

In all, Hoffman's relationship to the class had a therapeutic tinge: She spoke of her students' "connecting" to their material, urged them to find experiences in their own pasts to help them relate to the feelings expressed in the songs, and commented on parts of the singer's body which apparently had not been allowed to be as freely expressive as others. Interestingly, Hoffman's pedagogical style parallels on a dramatistic level the kind of "revelatory" aspect of much vocal training, whose implicit mission is to uncover, from underneath the tensions imposed by everyday bodily habits, the deep-lying propensity of the body to sing.

Hoffman's method of handling her student singers' sense of vulnerability at the crook of the piano may be contrasted with Lavane's approach. Lavane treated students' uneasiness as a function of stage fright, to be overcome by greater physical and thus mental concentration on the audience rather than on one's own technique, and dealt with bodily behavior most explicitly when stressing the communicative dimension of the recital. By contrast, Hoffman seemed to perceive any problems in expressivity in the traditional recital setting as related to the intrusion of the audience on the singer's concentration. When a singer had difficulty expressing the feeling implied in a song or making explicit its dramatic situation, Hoffman's interventions tended to encourage introspection in the student rather than increased physical extroversion.

One mezzo-soprano had difficulty relating to the blissfully confused emotional tone of the speaker in Schubert's "Lachen und Weinen" (Laughing and Crying), a song in which someone newly in love relates how she is inexplicably up one minute, down the next. Hoffman suggested that the singer repeat the song walking around the room, as if speaking wonderingly to herself. By removing the performance imperative, Hoffman seemed to be attempting to restore the sense of privacy which would prevail in the actual sensation of this strange emotion. Whereas Lavane's intervention would look to enriching communication between singer and audience, Hoffman seemed to assume that enhancing the contact between the singer and the material would lead to greater expressivity within the performance.

In a sense, Hoffman seemed to try to translate the performance conventions of the concert stage into those of the naturalistic drama, in
which the performer focuses first on strengthening his own empathy with
the material and then on cementing his relationships with the other
onstage characters (and not at all on clarifying the relationship with the
audience). It is as though drama were conceived of as a baseline form to
the art song concert, as a primitive origin and source of direction to which
concert singers may return for artistic nourishment.

A soprano singing Wolf's "Nun wandre, Maria," Joseph's song of
quiet encouragement to the exhausted and very pregnant Mary, seemed
to have difficulty bringing her body into play in expressing the mood and
action of the song. Hoffman asked her to enact the dramatic situation
suggested by the song. Choosing another student in the class to serve as
Mary, Hoffman directed the soprano to walk around the classroom, with
her arm around this "Mary," and to sing Wolf's song directly to her.
Somewhat humorously, the singer scoffed in apparent chagrin at the suggestion that the acting exercise actually take her away from the piano;
she did as directed with some resistance. Hoffman directed her to concentrate on the person she was singing to: "See her suffering, and let that
have an effect on you."

Like Lavane, Hoffman spoke about the dramatic use of the breath,
but framed its use in terms of the actions of the character of a song rather
than in terms of the communicative act. Here, she combined the
naturalistic drama concept of the objective with the stylistic conventions
of singing. She urged a soprano performing Ned Rorem's "The Silver
Swan" to "think of an active verb that will help you to use the breath expressively—to sign, to moan, to cry, and so on." Here, the singer chose
from a range of objectives (which can be expressed by an infinitive verb)
which are congruent with the notion of using the breath as dramatic action. Soliloquizing through song thus centers on singing as a dramatic action of its own. In a 1987 lecture on the boundary between music-theatre
and opera, German opera impresario and director August Everding reinforced this linking of the dramatic objective and the stylization of singing
by maintaining that performers learn their characters by discovering what
in them can be expressed only through singing, so that nothing will then
seem unnatural.

Finally, we should note in Hoffman's pedagogical style the contrast between the level of physical behavior she actually demanded from her students and her use of physical metaphors in her discussion of performance problems, her own movement about the room as she coached singers, and her insistence that singers do movement exercises to enable them better to connect with the material. To the singer working on "The Silver Swan," Hoffman pointed out that "It would be more poignant if something in you were *to reach out to it*, to long or yearn for Death to come close your eyes." As the singer tried on this idea in the song, Hoffman strenuously reached her own arm to point toward the back of the classroom, as if to indicate the distance to be bridged between the persona of the song and Death, yet there was no perceptible difference in the student's own motion toward that specific goal. If there was an alteration in the singer's conception of the song, it was virtual, not made manifest.

Despite Paul Sperry's overtly theatrical concert style, in his classes in Twentieth-Century Song and American Song at the Juilliard School of Music and in Song Interpretation at the Aspen Music Festival he dealt with interpretation more through pure musicianship than did either Lavane or Hoffman. Primarily, Sperry seemed to teach that the character of a song can best be approached by fidelity to the composer's tempo markings, and he frequently stopped his students at Juilliard (many of whom are semi-professional singers) for correction on problems of rhythm or tempo. Like a true exponent of the *Affektenlehre*, Sperry wants to unmask the dramatic basis of tempo markings. He refers to the "character" of a particular tempo as a guideline for performance, stressing that the singer must scrupulously adhere to the rhythm and tempo of a piece in order for the action of the song to emerge clearly. Of special importance when learning a song is the stage at which one pinpoints the differences between the poetic rhythm of the words and the rhythm in which the composer has chosen to set the song; it is here that one comes close to understanding the composer's conception of the poem he is setting. (Sperry recommends that when studying a new piece, singers first learn the poem entirely independently of the music, in its own rhythm; then learn to speak the poem in the given rhythm of the song; and only last learn the pitches of the song, which he considers the most straightforward part of the process.) In songs which depict or illustrate the motion of a being or object—such as a rocking cradle or a spinning wheel—it is of special necessity that the temporal choices of the performance convey the proper motion.

Sperry reinforced his students not for specific physical or gestural choices they made in the performance of a song, but for extremely general values—if they displayed energy, enthusiasm, even extravagance in their approach to a work. At times, his singers seemed to perform these very qualities, especially when repeating a song under Sperry's close direction, rather than subsuming their attention within the action of the song. The result was a performance which stressed—albeit at a more confident, pleasing level—the relationship of the singer to the act of performing rather than any more profound relationship to or through the material.

More than the other teachers, Sperry was willing—indeed, at times eager—to encourage his students to change their tone color and breathing style for a song, even in an unflattering way, to serve the character depicted in it. Sperry readily demonstrated various vocal choices for interpretation, though never a physical choice. This selection may be due in part to his perception of the song recital as an art form in which suggestion plays a vital role. He described a song in which the vocal persona narrates kicking another character downstairs. Sperry once saw the song performed with a literal, methodically executed kick, after which the singer drew a delicate handkerchief from his jacket pocket and carefully dusted the ousted's projected point of contact with his shoe. Sperry recalled his offense at the time at the "specificity" of the gesture, and in retrospect judged that such a literal dramatic choice detracts from an essential feature of the song recital as a genre of suggestion, able to evoke in the listener's imagination—rather than to visually depict—the events, emotions, and characters of a song.

There are a number of issues raised by the pedagogical styles of these instructors of interpretation. While certain physical behaviors may be engendered and perpetuated by the process of learning songs, they may also be substantially influenced by the instructional system, which bears on the singer's visual focus and his use, as "marking" devices, of facial expression, gesture, and body tonicity and readiness to respond. First, the process of learning new material is essentially one which for a long time binds the singer's eyes to a written score. Early rehearsals of a piece in class or in a professional setting often take place with music stand in place

and the singer's eyes focused on reading the music rather than on projecting it to an audience. When combined with many voice teachers' custom
of training the singer's face to remain impassive to permit the "free"
production of sound, the process of learning music helps to create a
deadened, held face, even after the removal of the music stand.

In addition, teachers' comments and corrections may be internalized
and put into use by the singer during the labored period in which all his
physical attention is placed on learning the music, during a time in which
the body is not open to discovering physical correlates to musically
couched suggestions, much less able to put any more directly physical
suggestions into free use since a music stand blocks his contact with the
audience. Singers often attempt to attain visual independence of the
score by inculcating the musical features of the work in their bodies,
usually "conducting" themselves, as I described earlier, with pliés and little motions of their arms. Note that the parts of the bodies which are freely moved are those that are not usually conceived of as being intimately
bound up with the singing process.

Even in the absence of score and music, tight visual contact between instructor and student may produce another set of behaviors, in
which some aspect of the performance is "marked." In some cases, a
dominant facial expression will be marked, even in advance of the beginning of the song, and held throughout the song, with peculiar effect. One
singer in Hoffman's class set her face in a particular emotional expression,
as if donning a mask, before singing the Brahms love song, "Dein blaues
Augen." Her blocking of motion in her face extended even to the times
when she needed to instruct her accompanist in a more appropriate
tempo, as though she would be distracted from her task by breaking the
outward visual focus. Remaining facing out toward the class, she held her
face intently under the same mask as when singing, while directing the
pianist only by performing a circular "cranking" motion with her right
hand.

In other cases, a certain level of energy will be mirrored in the
teacher's behavior or performed for reinforcement from the teacher. Perhaps because of Sperry's habit of reinforcing students for energy and enthusiasm, energy itself was frequently marked in his classes. Explicit
marking also occurred in Hoffman and Lavane's students most often

when they requested that a student repeat a song with sidelines coaching from the instructor.

A third type of marking is simply the performance of attention to the teacher's response at various moments to the ongoing performance of the song. Singers appear to be especially sensitive to audience response and to "listen" for instructor response with their entire bodies during repetitions of songs in class or master class, in a manner rarely seen in their first renditions. They glance up to make contact with the teachers as they take in new breaths, shadow their instructors' conducting motions while looking straight ahead, and exchange smiles with instructor and fellow students immediately on having incorporated a suggestion. They appear to concentrate on receiving affirmation of their correct performance of instructors' suggestions, rather than on incorporating those suggestions smoothly into the overall design of the piece.

The public master class seems to be a genre peculiarly fitted to producing marking behaviors. The fact that most master classes in conservatories today are directed by touring stars of the opera and concert stage, now well into the second half of their careers, means that a pervasive element demonstrated in students' behavior is an exaggerated deference. Concentration during second and subsequent renditions of a song in a master class tends to be directed both toward eliciting affirmative signals from the master teacher that the student has performed the suggested change correctly and toward marking the suggestions themselves. The persistence of work behaviors in actual performance, to a large extent by student singers and less so by professionals, may thus be attributed at least in part to features of a learning process that is strongly visual and oriented not on the relationship between singer and audience so much as that between singer and teacher.

CHAPTER III

Deconstructions of the Recital

Operatic tenor Ira Siff is the artistic director of La Gran Scena Opera Company, an all-male company of singers who perform scenes from grand opera in falsetto and *en travestie*. Siff himself has created a Ukrainian female opera star persona, Vera Galupe-Borszkh, around whom he has developed a series of "annual farewell" recital programs which he performs in Manhattan clubs. In concert with pianist Ross Barentyne (who has taken the stage name Maestro Francesco Folinari-Soave-Coglioni), Siff sings—for a largely gay, entirely enthusiastic male audience—arias from the standard repertoire, as well as an occasional art song. In his performance we will examine characteristic gestural choices, particular to the type of persona Siff has created, as well as more situational and larger-scale issues: the audience-performer relationship, specifically with respect to the audience's adulation of the performer (as has been the case historically and to a lesser extent today when opera singers present art song recitals); the use of costume and the staging of costume changes as dramatic devices; the shaping and the musicalization of introductions and transitions between numbers; as well as questions raised by the "contamination" of the usually vessel-like recital performer by a clear-cut, admittedly flamboyant persona.

The work of John Kelly, a New York performance artist specializing in austere, precisely choreographed works based on subjects from art and music history, will provide the other case study of a contemporary elaboration on the recital tradition. A solo performer, Kelly usually sings in falsetto with taped orchestra accompaniment. *Born With the Moon in*

Ira Siff as Madame Vera Galupe-Borszkh in one of many Annual Farewell
Recitals. (Photo by Daniel Eifert)

Cancer is a performance art piece created in 1986 in which Kelly performs a starkly choreographed song recital with added—though minimal—props, settings, and costume. The work will furnish the basis of a discussion of the staging and physical translation of songs; the viable deconstructions of recital stage conventions and their effects; the choreographic transmutation of the emotional qualities of songs; and the significance of an aural learning process when combined with a kinetic and visual approach to musical performance.

Mme. Vera Galupe-Borszkh's cabaret act at Don't Tell Mama, entitled "The Second Annual Farewell Recitals," openly advertises these transitional moments as part of its attraction. An announcement of the performances reads, "Join the beloved still-singing soprano as she shares gems from her vast repertoire. And, between selections, Madame 'tells all,' illuminating her life and career through the art of The Diva Anecdote." In the act, Siff's operatic persona assesses her competitors, shares tales of her family life in Russia (with Great Uncle Sergei and Tchaikovsky), explains the appeal of the recital setting for her (*no other singers!*), and opines on the takeover of opera by method actors and modern directors.

What the creator of Galupe-Borszkh, Ira Siff, terms the Diva Anecdote is a flamboyant element peculiar to opera singers who perform in recital, for whom the recital setting is an unusual and welcome kind of intimacy unavailable to them on the opera stage. The recital platform becomes for opera singers an opportunity to reveal to an infatuated audience a favored image of themselves. In Galupe-Borszkh's recital, transitional anecdotes illustrate the performer's emphatic relation to the audience. Unlike the singer of art song, Galupe-Borszkh treats the audience as an active interlocutor which substitutes for any stage partners. Singing the aria "Son Vergin Vezzosa" from Bellini's *I Puritani*, Galupe-Borszkh uses repetitions of her assertion of sexual purity as indignant counters to the imagined challenges of audience members.

Unlike the singer of art song in recital, this performer refuses to play alone. If she cannot pass the audience off as partner, Galupe-Borszkh creates silent, invisible interlocutors to play opposite her onstage. In the lament, "When I am Laid in Earth" from Purcell's *Dido and Aeneas*, Dido sings to her maid Belinda of her approaching death and the meaning she hopes it will have for those who survive her. Imploring that Belinda lend her her hand for strength, Galupe-Borszkh reaches out and sandwiches an invisible hand between her own, holding all three in the air for the better part of the aria. Later, she nestles her head on Belinda's invisible bosom, and mouths a humble "thank you" up at her.

Galupe-Borszkh's transformation of the cabaret audience into partner and her manufacture of onstage interlocutors exemplify this singing persona's doggedly dramatic approach to the recital setting, and creates the context for her dramatization (or perhaps, operatization) even of moments which are not inherently dramatic, as in the lyrical expression of the Tchaikovsky song (of Uncle Sergei's) entitled "Utchevwaw?" ("Why?"). The song consists of a series of ponderings of nature's mysteries, which become a metaphor for the singer's culminating ruminations about love. In a more standard recital format, the singer might underscore by quiescence the melancholically musing quality of the song, yet Galupe-Borszkh makes even this lyrical expression a dynamic, dramatic one. During "Utchevwaw's" interludes, she indicates silently and repeatedly, through exaggerated, all-consuming facial expressions, the question, "Why?" She draws her eyes together tautly and gazes with childlike quizzicality at the audience. By keeping the question "Why?" a dynamic, honestly inquisitive one which depends on the audience as interlocutor, the singer renders an originally lyrical expression dramatic. Similarly, Galupe-Borszkh transforms into a more interactive, dramatic moment Dido's repeated injunction to Belinda to "Remember me, but forget my fate." She renders the repeated "Remember me's" as questions, taking them wholly out of the context of the aria. The soprano demands of the audience frantically, "Remember me?" She trots round the side of the piano and directs her question at her accompanist, who glances up dumbly from the piano and nods; she appears reassured.

On a larger scale than the verbal and musical, Galupe-Borszkh costumes and stages her arias and songs as if she were performing them on a grand opera stage. She changes into a disheveled wig and lays a basket of flowers over her arm when performing Ophelia from Thomas's *Hamlet*. She affects a wedding gown and carries a white bouquet, which she tosses into the audience at the end of her first act opener, "Son Vergin Vezzosa." She performs a Wolf song, "Die Zigeunerin" ("The Gypsy"), which presents in dialogue two characters, a gypsy and her suitor, not as suggestions but as literal impersonations. Racing during the interludes between center stage and stage right to play the different characters, Galupe-Borszkh also devises contrasting physical styles for the two figures. Her gypsy rests one hand languidly on the piano, the other hand on her outshot hip. Her mouth is never inactive: When she's not singing during this song, she rotates her eyelids and lips seductively outward toward the audience. The suitor, on the other hand, is like a five-year-old with his first pop gun; flapping his flaccid forearms, this character manically argues that since he can shoot an animal, he can capture a gypsy, easy.

Perhaps in homage to Felsenstein, opera director August Everding advised young opera singers that, when learning roles, they should discover what about the character can only live or express himself through singing—then nothing that happens in opera can seem unnatural. Mme. Vera Galupe-Borszkh is herself such a character, one who can only exist on the opera stage. She introduces the Mad Scene from *Hamlet*, and adds that Hamlet's aria "Essere or [sic] non essere" ("To be or not to be") is an "optional cut." In pronounced relief against the greater passivity of the recital singer, Galupe-Borszkh positively infects her performance with her feverish empathy for her characters. As she provides the translations to her arias before singing them, she often rehearses alongside them the physical attitudes which express her words. While translating literally the more lyrical art songs (which she performs rather faithfully), she quite loosely paraphrases the language of opera arias, very much in her own responsive idiom and adding in what ought to occur in stage behavior during the aria as though it were an integral part of the lyrical text.

Aksel Schiøtz contended that "To interpret actually means to explain. Thus the singer should explain to his audience the contents of a poem by way of music" (Schiøtz 1970, 20). For this Ukrainian soprano "who has only been in this country twelve years," the illustration of meaning becomes an essential part of her performance style. Galupe-Borszkh illustrates specific words, both as she translates her selections and while singing them, as if signifying their meaning in speech to a native who could not understand her tourist tongue. She sings the Italian word for "justice" impersonating the symbolic scales.

The singer demonstrates the amplified, clumsily impassioned gestural behavior appropriate to the expression of the sentiments she sings as if they had merely been spoken. Her very literalism, so eager, is what is fetching. Singing of impending death, she begins to work without moving her lips, blinking, or contracting any of her facial muscles: she literally deadens.

Even vocal behavior becomes a kind of physical gesture for this singer who, in Everding's terms, finds a way to live through music. Singing her final, the obligatory "popular," number, McBroom's "The Rose" (sung by Bette Midler in the film of the same name), Galupe-Borszkh animates nonverbal and verbal singing as utterances from two separate musical streams. She sings her final musical cadenza on a vowel, lifting her left hand, and "voices" her climaxing phrase, "The Rose," extending her right toward the audience. Trills become bleary-eyed contests between two warring points of visual focus.

Despite her detestation of method actors and modern directors, Galupe-Borszkh has apparently internalized the teachings of opera director and trainer Boris Goldovsky, who required singers to find ways to "use" all of the music. When reciting the poetry of her songs during transitions between songs, Galupe-Borszkh even adds in the nonverbal vocalizations, the "la's" and the "hey's," which she speaks in the syncopated rhythm in which they may be set by the composer, directing an expression to the audience indicating the considerable significance of these so-called "nonsense" syllables.

Preludes and postludes are no less meaningful for this vocal persona. In the "Thpanith" song which is Galupe-Borszkh's first encore, the extended prelude represents the singer's repeated and frustrated attempts to speak. She opens her mouth to express an idea, checks it, reshapes it, and tries again in a different way, only finally to succeed when the score permits. The postlude to "Dido's Lament" shows us Dido's actual death, performed in rhythm with the music, a succession of sudden collapses and labored efforts to continue to sing (or, as time goes on, to die in the attempt to sing).

Galupe-Borszkh's recital displays the contamination of the singer-as-receptacle by an undauntable singer persona. In her, the recitalist is no longer made accessible and charismatic to the audience through what

Wesley Balk describes as a vulnerability and openness to the different characters, but by her mapping of her own unmistakable personality onto them. Siff's creation of the character of Galupe-Borszkh teaches us about the play of persona when well-known opera singers perform in recitals. Even in these cases—where parody is not the central event—personality and persona play a much more prominent role than in the preferred decorum of the art song recital. Galupe-Borszkh is her own attraction, not her musical selections per se—though the singing displays admirable musicianship. In particular, the cabaret act is geared to attract a predominantly gay male audience, not only through Siff's transvestite performance, but also through numerous malapropisms in the character's Diva Anecdotes, which serve as "inadvertent" sexual come-ons or jokes, e.g., "Thank you for coming to the Second Annual Farewell Recital. I can tell already it will be a pleasure performing on you. . . . My next selection will be 'When I Am Laid.' " Despite the fruitful issues raised on the subject of physical performance in her recital, Galupe-Borszkh's cabaret work may have more primarily to do with audience-performer interaction and mutual affirmation in a common identity—not so much as *music* lovers but as *potential* lovers. In her cabaret show, Galupe-Borszkh radically redefines the meaning of the singer's requisite accessibility.

Performance artist John Kelly's work *Born With the Moon in Cancer* shares with Galupe-Borszkh's act the sense of heartsmitten operatic parody. With changes of costume, a single prop and set piece, and abstract movement Kelly performs a solo voice recital in falsetto range. As in a more orthodox recital, Kelly does not speak. However, he has created minimalistic, highly gestural choreography to interpret the orchestral overtures and preludes to the works he sings. The selections are from the classical repertoire, most of them Italian arias, though he also performs works in French, a fractured German, and English. All the foreign languages, and even the English, have varying degrees of gibberish thrown in, for several reasons. First, Kelly did not read music, nor did he understand much French or German, and learnt music by ear, by listening to the recordings of others. Second, in the week's preparation that he had before the first performance of the work, he did not have the time to learn the words on his own, and did not work with a musical coach on the languages. Finally and most important, he viewed the words as mere "vehicles to get to another place" anyhow: Since he felt all of the pieces

John Kelly in *Born With the Moon in Cancer* (Photo by Dona Ann McAdams)

he performed display a different emotional "quality," Kelly was able to set the works in an order that made intuitive sense to him.

Although Kelly now has a reputation as a choreographer, he considers the movement in *Born With the Moon in Cancer* to be minimal. It is "almost just an accompaniment to the singing, . . . like a staged concert." He considers the singing, and the emotional communication that issues from it, to be the key element in the work. Kelly's choreographic choices in *Born With the Moon in Cancer* are economically bound up with his tagging of the songs with specific "qualities." Whereas Galupe-Borszkh illustrated particular words on a strict meaning level, Kelly often performs a single abstracted quality of a song throughout. This quality may be a stylized representation of the principal emotion depicted in the song or a repetition of the central dramatic action or of an image of a character. Exemplifying the emotional self-display of the character in Carmen's "Habañera," for example, Kelly sings in a gold lamé wrap jumpsuit, step-crossing lightly with jazzy little steps and mild hip swings. Here, Kelly wears blinders, the nail polish-painted goggles which together with the jumpsuit make his body look like an otherworldly creature, a bug with the sophistication of Nature.

As Dalilah pleads in the Saint-Saëns aria that Samson caress her, Kelly interlaces his fingers as if in supplication, a gestural reproduction of the principal overt dramatic action of the aria (actually, Dalilah is seducing Samson to weaken him, in order to find out the secret of his strength). Keeping his hands thus interlocked, Kelly experiments with the abstract movement possibilities of the dramatically meaningful position. He swings his hands down heavily from the shoulder, as if batting a low ball, and repeats the movement on alternating sides. Holding his palms parallel to the floor and wringing his hands, he carries a rippling wave motion from one arm up the other and back. The overall effect is like that of a roller-coaster.

Finally, Pergolesi's "Se tu m'ami, se sospiri" ("If you loved and sighed for me"), for example, is the coy song of a shepherdess to her lover. Shading his painted eyes as if against the noonday mountain sun, Kelly performs the characteristic searching attitude of the shepherdess as a distilled gestural essence of scanning the hills—not for sheep, but for a suitable (other) husband, should this one not succumb.

At the beginning of *Born With the Moon in Cancer*, Kelly enters from the back of the room, a long chiffon scarf tied as a blindfold around his eyes and billowing long behind him. Throughout most of the work, Kelly's eyes are stylized or refigured in some way. Once he removes the scarf, he performs with his eyes shut. I ponder the masklike effect of a pair of childlike, somehow Pierrot-like eyes painted open on his closed eyelids. Later in the work, he goes backstage to change into the gold lamé jumpsuit for the "Habañera" and returns to the stage with black and white eyes painted on the front of a pair of goggles. Toward the end of the piece, wearing only the long top to a pair of long johns, Kelly wipes the make-up violently off his eyes and performs for the first time in his own face, unstylized and triangular. Since interpretation teachers, such as Lavane, emphasize the importance of the eyes as among the chief expressive equipment of the recitalist, the fact that Kelly immobilizes his own eyes for most of the performance is quite significant. Offensive to some opera singers who have seen him perform (and walked out because of the way he clearly mangles his throat in order to produce the sounds he imitates by ear), Kelly's mouth is exceptionally expressive for a singer of this repertoire.

Other, equally sparse production elements in the work seem to have narrative significance as well. The songs and arias are strung together as if part of a song cycle—and all are addressed to a large stuffed chicken, the visible counterpart of Galupe-Borszkh's silent interlocutors. Interestingly enough, invisible, Galupe-Borszkh's "answer back"; visible, Kelly's remains silent. As the piece progresses, Kelly caresses and scratches this chicken, singing a coy early Italian love aria to it; gives it a ride in the sole piece of furniture, a rotating office chair; gives it its independence; seduces it with Dalilah's smouldering "Mon coeur s'ouvre at ta voix" ("My heart opens at the sound of your voice"), and, in the end, mourns its death. The chicken is a curious love object, a nonjudgmental presence whose constancy nevertheless ties the work together as an impressionistically narrative one. In using the chicken and relationship-centered emotion to structure *Born With the Moon* narrativically, Kelly has given the recital a tinge of operatic design. Although Kelly has constructed the piece as a stylization of an autobiographical narrative, any story is for the spectator secondary to Kelly's compellingly musical falsetto renditions of these works, to his ascetic figure, and to his abstract physical performance within the recital setting.

Kelly changes some element of his costume or make-up design for almost every song in the recital, a feature which has its historical precedent in some of the concert singers of the early twentieth century who kept and often made their own extensive costume collections. Yvette Guilbert, for example, believed that songs should, whenever possible, be performed in period dress (1918). Ursula Greville stressed the use of costume so much in her interview with Frederick Martens that he entitled it "The Frock as a Factor in Concert Success." Greville used costumes for suggestions of character and to suggest the mood of a song, but always with a mind to comfort in singing:

> I never bother to get the exact period frock for in those days I'm sure there were women who refused to follow fashion, and altered the period frocks, just as they do to-day. It is the suggestion which counts. To begin with, it would be impossible to sing in many of the garments owing to the restriction. I could spend hours on this subject, which I believe to be a most important factor in getting the man in the street interested visually as well as aurally (Greville 1923, 137).

Choreographically, *Born With the Moon in Cancer* centers on a signature series of four musically phrased, punctual motivic gestures, which are repeated as refrains of a kind at various points in the recital for four- or eight-beat phrases each. In the first movement, Kelly draws the pointed index fingers of each hand up laterally by the sides of his head, then heavily and emphatically points down toward the ground in front of him. In the second movement, he rests one forearm on another as if cradling a baby, and rocks his arms first left, then right, left, right. The movement is precise and mechanical. It loses momentum and stops crankily at its highest point on each side. The third movement consists of crossing the left arm stiffly across the body, while the right hand, flat, is raised at a right angle to the upper arm. The eyebrows are raised and held, almost maniacally. The fourth movement Kelly takes walking birdlike in a circle, picking his feet up stickily from the ground, his body bent forward at a thirty-degree angle, his chin jutting forward. He places the backs of his wrists against his shoulder blades and flaps his hands.

This fourth motivic movement is not the only one in the piece in which Kelly seems to mimic or even to become the chicken which is the apparent object of his love. At other moments, Kelly bends forward slightly from the shoulders and moves his head suddenly, with quick, irregular changes of focus. Indeed, the theme of reflexivity and role exchange—and not only on the level of gender—is one which pervades Kelly's work altogether. In an earlier piece, *The Dagmar Onassis Story*, Kelly lip-synchs as accompaniment to a film of himself playing Maria Callas, his operatic inspiration. At one point in the film, he shuts her voice out of the recording and sings as if for her so that, in effect, she is lip-synching to his voice. Kelly explains: "I supplied her with my voice, since she was dead." And, Kelly reports, though he rarely went to the opera, he listened to recordings, especially of Callas, as much as he could. "I loved opera so much, I wanted to become it. And lip-synching was just one way of taking it into your body and being kinetic about it, but emoting" (Kelly interview 1988).

Although Kelly is interested in taking on characters, especially androgynous "creatures from someplace," in *Born With the Moon* he feels that he is playing different aspects of himself. He asserted, "The character doesn't have a name, it's me: It's like a concert in that way." Although he works with a personal subtextual story line, there is a sound resemblance between the way he conceives of this work and the prevailing conception of the recital singer as being completely pliant. Kelly's virtuosic malleability—physical, visual, and musical—is example enough of such elasticity.

Born in Jersey City, John Kelly began performing shortly after high school, soon after he accepted a full scholarship at the American Ballet Theater School. The son of a visual artist, Kelly had always assumed that he would take on that role himself, and wavered between an identity as a dancer and one as a visual artist, taking up fashion illustration at the Parsons School of Design in New York and completing a bachelor's degree there. After seeing a drag queen lip-synch to a Nina Hagen record in a Greenwich Village club, Kelly began to perform, outlandishly outfitted, as a club lip-syncher himself, combining his talents as professional dancer and designer. He only began to sing in the mid-'80s, though he had always known that "my falsetto had a personality to it" (Kelly interview

1988). Up to the late 1980s, Kelly was an untrained countertenor with extraordinary musicality and a voice others encouraged him to develop for more conventional opera work. His transition from being a silent to a sound artist he views as a turning point in his artistic life. This transition plays a critical role in the subtext of *Born With the Moon in Cancer*, which Kelly has also presented under the name *The Discovery of Sound*.

For the most part in this deconstructed recital, Kelly's gestures are symmetrical, like those of the more conventional recitalist. Indeed, he often layers such stock gestures over his song, with little regard for meaning. He clasps his hands over his breast, opens his arms wide at his sides, extends them low toward the audience in an imploring manner, and stretches them Christlike down at his sides, shoulders and palms pressed forward. Unlike the classically trained singer, Kelly is willing to place his hands, still in a symmetrical position, close to his mouth and face. He clasps his cheeks and temples as if his senses had utterly abandoned him.

Occasionally, Kelly's movements evoke cultural stereotypes of the language in which he sings; he colors an Italian aria, for example, curling his fingers back under the side of his jaw and then extending his forearm forward. Like Galupe-Borszkh, Kelly mixes a prosaic, speechlike gestural style side-by-side with a more self-aggrandizing, parodically noble stock gesture. Kelly's musical variation on the prosaic is his repetition of everyday speech gestures throughout a sung phrase. However, the dynamism of repetition itself is unusual in his work: Kelly thrives on the gesture that is a "punctuation mark," which physically sums up the mood or quality he wishes to communicate to the audience. In general, he shifts position to a new tableau with the first downbeat of a new musical phrase and holds the position and attitude throughout the phrase.

Kelly's penchant for the attitude he attributes not only for his distaste for the "gratuitous movement" of much of contemporary choreography, but more importantly to his experience as a visual artist working from models who took "compelling poses" which he then had to "render." He has himself also worked as an artist's model. In Kelly's own career, "rendering" has become transferred from the realm of visual interpretation to that of enactment and embodiment. It is important to remark Kelly's patterning of gesture for musical performance on visual models, similar to eighteenth-century acting style, which, as I outlined in chapter 1, caused

performers to refer to painting and sculpture for models for physical attitudes.

Kelly's experience as a lip-syncher, when coupled with his solely
aural learning process once he actually began to sing in public, contrasts
with the substantially visual learning process of conventional recitalists,
outlined in the previous chapter. While traditional singers deaden and
freeze the body in order first to learn to produce tone and then lock the
expressive qualities of their eyes as they concentrate physical energy on
reading the music, as a lip-syncher Kelly began as a performer aiming to
give a body to sound. Working as his own director, choreographer, and
teacher, there can be no imitative or emotion-blocking marking in Kelly's
learning process. Indeed, the very "blinding" of his own eyes for most of
the performance, though it also serves a narrative purpose, highlights all
of the other parts of the performing body, including and perhaps especially his mouth; the stylistic choice of blinders obliterates the traditional
recitalist's usual reliance on the eyes for expression, while deemphasizing
the mouth as a working instrument.

Kelly's reshaping of the singing body parallels an important trend in
twentieth-century mime. For the post-naturalism twentieth-century
mime, the particularity of expression in mimicry became a standard
against which to rebel. Mimes such as Etienne Decroux and Jean-Louis
Barrault donned a neutral cosmetic mask, or one which expressed a single
emotion, and performed without music, relying on the more abstract
movements of the body to convey a dramatic idea. The deemphasis of the
face and of the musical aspects of mimic movement carried twentieth-
century mime further away from the predominantly facial solutions to
problems of dramatic interpretation in recital singing (Dorcy 1961, 32).

The superposition of abstract dance gesture on top of the songs
makes Kelly, in Cone's terms, a persona who may well express himself
through dance but who may not know that he can and does sing.
Through such consciousness, the choreography thus locates Kelly more
than the conventional recitalist at the center of a profound aestheticism.
The choreography shows Kelly's interpretive embodiment of the characters who would perform these songs, as well as his assessment of them.
Performing half in English, half in *Fracturdeutsch* a version of Mozart's

"Die Alt" (The Old One), Kelly both mourns and satirizes the passing of a carefree period in gay sexual behavior and social life.

His staging of his songs over the stage space and his use of props, costumes, and set become in a sense Kelly's most radical deconstruction of the conventional recital. Kelly takes an active role toward the music. Where we as audience participate most is in our recognition of the recurring series of motivic gestures which functions as a kinetic, and somehow musical, refrain. We therefore focus not on the music, but on what it seems to mean to him physically, embodied. As an audience, we are offered principally a glimpse of a response to or interpretation of the music, within an overarching notion of emotional quality, rather than the music itself. In a sense, then, rather than being shared with the audience, the music remains throughout the show John Kelly's own.

CHAPTER IV

Closing Words: Gesture in Song

In the wake of a misapprehended Stanislavski, there is much facile talk by pedagogues about "spontaneity" and "naturalness" in physical interpretive style. What can be natural about playing twenty different characters, within as many musical conceptions, while standing rooted like a tree in one place? It is no wonder, since singers are given so little training within the recital's own conventions of style, that so many of them waver between standing motionlessly and moving self-consciously, or that they depend on stock gestures without knowing their meaning. Because of the inflexible, prescriptive general conventions of the recital, singers are hardly free to express themselves in the style of the naturalistic drama.

There must be a difference between a style of performance in which a character's only means of making a difference in his external world lies in musical and verbal actions and that style of performance—for example, staged drama—in which physical actions can have an impact on a character's world. While physical behavior obviously plays a role in the audience's *perception* of character and situation, in song recital physical behavior is better characterized as expression than as action: Its realm of effect lies in the inner rather than in the outer world.

The inner world of song is indissolubly wedded with private gesture. In accord with oral interpretation author Chester Clayton Long, Edward Cone asserted that the text—in his case, a musical one—is a map of gestural "utterances":

It is the gestural aspect of utterance that is simulated, and symbolized, by music. If music is a language at all, it is a language of gesture: of direct actions, of pauses, of startings and stoppings, of rises and falls, of tenseness and slackness, of accentuations. . . .

The gestures of music can be interpreted as symbolic of physical as well as verbal gestures. For a physical gesture is an action that emulates an utterance—an action that tries to speak (hence our admiration of the "eloquent" gesture). If music resembles utterance in being sound, it resembles physical gesture by being speechless. Once more, in music symbolic utterance and symbolic gesture come together. Indeed, in music symbolic utterance is symbolic gesture (Cone 1974, 164–65).

Cone stated further that the relationship between gesture and meaning depends on context, rather than the two being deterministically paired: "No context, no content" (Cone 1974, 165). Although he seems to allot a privileged place to physical gesture, Cone actually posed the verbal as the irreducible substratum to both physical and musical gesture, since music represents physical gesture and physical gesture emulates speech. Yet gesture does not succeed in replacing speech: Musical and verbal utterance meet with gesture at the symbolic, not at the actual level. The song recital, if we are to agree with Cone, stresses a more profound meaning which commonly undergirds the verbal, the musical, and the physical—and that meaning may be found in the inner world or in the artistry of the performer.

Paul Souriau related that in observing human behavior, one can choose to attend to another's experience of emotion, to observe his physical expression of that emotion, or to compare the relationship between the two, seeing how emotion may be enacted physically. One tends, he maintained, to examine and judge the physical depiction of emotion in, for example, studying expressive movements or the attitudes of statues (Souriau 1983, 101). The performing arts altogether are continually subject, even at an unconscious level, to such aesthetic comparisons between their inner life and their outward expression.

Winn stated that by the doctrine of the *Affektenlehre* mere accuracy was appraised as the lowest, though appreciable, level of imitation; the imitation of beautiful objects was regarded higher yet and higher still was the imitation of beautiful objects with emotional meaning. He maintained that where music can only be truly imitative is in its ability to evoke sounds, as in the call of a bird, or motion, as in the running and lapping of a stream. Indeed, as Daniel Webb postulated in his eighteenth-century *Observations on the Correspondence Between Poetry and Music*, the "central metaphor on which the *Affektenlehre* was based was an equation of motion and emotion":

> As we have no direct nor immediate knowledge of the mechanical operations of the passions, we endeavour to form some conception of them from the manner in which we find ourselves affected by them: thus we say, that love softens, melts, insinuates; anger quickens, stimulates, inflames; pride expands, exalts; sorrow dejects, relaxes: of all which ideas we are to observe, that they are different modifications of motion, so applied as best to correspond with our feelings of each particular passion. From whence, as well as from their known and visible effects, there is just reason to presume, that the passions, according to their several natures, do produce certain proper and distinctive motions in the most refined and subtle parts of the human body. What these parts are, where placed, or how fitted to receive and propagate these motions, are points which I shall not inquire into. . . .
>
> I shall suppose, that it is in the nature of music to excite similar vibrations, to communicate similar movements to the nerves and spirits. For, if music owes its being to motion, and, if passion cannot well be conceived to exist without it, we have a right to conclude, that the agreement of music with passion can have no other origin than a coincidence of movements (Winn 1982, 232–33).

Webb reasoned that both music and emotion find their counterparts in motion. Yet in life emotions do not alter as nimbly as motion. In time, they grow and soften, acquire different shadings, and our perspective on them may change. In songs, emotions change even more slowly. Since music is generally thought of as a means of extending time, it is important to point out that such extension has the effect of causing us to perform or examine, in each musical moment, the inner life of the vocal persona in finer detail than we could in ordinary time. Opera is commonly believed to deal in generalized emotions, perhaps because of its stripped-down libretti. Because we have through musical time the opportunity, however, to look at each moment multiplied in time and in profuse, excruciating emotional detail, opera and vocal music generally treat emotion in a more minute, not a more general, manner than does life. The profusion of

detail contributes to our sense that emotion in vocal music is more intense than in life—a different matter altogether from scope.

A given art song portrays not a succession of emotions, but rather a
single or a simple complex of emotions. If motion continues throughout a
song, what can it be imitating along the way, even if the overall object of
imitation is emotion?

In an essay entitled "The Poetic Halo," Marcel Marceau wrote that

> A gesture, unless lyrically sustained, is but a drawing in space. Still, it is
> necessary to measure and situate it in time by giving it dramatic power. This
> power will either prove poetical, or will contrast brutally with its outline,
> leaving only a spasm, a jolt, a break, a straight line or curve, a kind of cold
> and linear geometry.
>
> A gesture is not sufficient; it needs to be clothed in a thought. And
> the drawing which expresses this thought must be accurate. Finally, the
> *style* must stand out. . . .
>
> When the actor-mime sustains his dramatic action with the inspira-
> tion of his thought, the sensitive response he induces is the echo of his soul,
> and the gesture becomes a silent inner song. The actor-mime *vibrates* like
> the strings of a harp. He is *lyrical: his gesture seems to be invested with a poetic
> halo* (Dorcy 1961, 103–4).

Marceau's likening of excellence in mimic gesture to song bears cogently
on our present project. It is gesture's interdependence with thought and
not its sterile beauty which the great mime champions and which he identifies as being songlike; thus, song and the highest form of gesture are
alike held to express the thought process of the presented persona, or the
attitude of the performer toward his material. Given the perhaps not-so-
subtle extent to which in chapter 2 I privileged "world" gestures in recital
singing over "work" gestures, my own similar prejudice toward thought-
motivated movement was likely revealed. Yet the subject of this book
would probably present itself far less pressingly for study if gestures that
were not motivated by thought—that either of the vocal persona or of
the performer—were less prevalent in the performance of song recitals. It
is precisely because we often notice a formal discrepancy between the
theme or words of a song and the gestural style of the performer that we,
along with Marceau, can make a distinction between "drawing" gestures
and thought-related ones, where thought is taken to be the cognitive

process of the vocal persona or the performer as he works through some aspect of the content of the song.

For Marceau, gesture fused with thought becomes a "silent inner song." Although he phrased his definition in an imagistic, metaphorical fashion, we may still regard it as containing the kernel of his concept of ideal gesture. Whether we take "silent inner song" to represent Marceau's "poetic halo," construe it to mean more literally gesture that possesses a musical quality, or view it as a poetic means of expressing his notion of artistic emotion, our conclusions will be similar. Song is all these things: music, poetic art in the shape of lyric, and embodied, performed emotion. In Marceau's metaphoric model, what underpins ideal mimic gesture and makes it songlike is its connection with thought.

Other writers, teachers, and performers have viewed physical aspects of performance in song recitals as imitating the movement of thoughts and emotions. In chapter 1, we saw how Aksel Schiøtz presented the recital as a chance to "explain" poetry to an audience by way of music, proposing a cognitive model of song performance. Schiøtz's view of song performance reproduces the eighteenth-century's goading that individual performers relate powerfully to the audience.

Here we may look once again to Mme. Vera Galupe-Borszkh's cabaret show, in light of the gestural category Ekman designated illustrators, first defined here in chapter 2 as movements which are intimately tied to the content and/or flow of speech (Ekman 1977, 49). Galupe-Borszkh is constantly in extravagant physical motion, demonstrating the meanings of words. The majority of her illustrative gestures fall under Ekman's category of pictographs. She draws in the air or acts out the shape of the referent as if she were engaged in *speech* rather than in song, and with a person who did not understand her language. The vocal trills which she performs by alternating with increasing speed between two points of visual focus are also pictographs and what she paints in the air the literal musical content of her scores.

By acting out word meanings, the singer is demonstrating the content of thought rather than its flow. Her dwelling on content is one of the factors that distinguishes this parodic singing persona from the more understating professional singer. Elisabeth Schwarzkopf, for example, moves almost imperceptibly during the postlude of Schubert's "An die Musik"

("Ode to Music"). Remaining in character, she shifts her focus slightly to the right, then ever-so-subtly back to center as the piece comes to an end; it is as though she is responding, thoughtfully and in musical time, to her own act of utterance. In contrast with Galupe-Borszkh's preoccupation with content, we see in Schwarzkopf's recital the body responding to the flow of thought. Her movement is, in Ekman's terms, ideographic—sketching the shape or path of thought, which is itself always in motion. Christa Ludwig concentrates on limited body parts—namely the mouth and eyes—to convey the meaning of her songs, and insists that if her stage lighting reveal nothing else, it should highlight the movements of these parts. Her mouth communicates the words to the audience and her eyes her response to them, imitating—or more accurately, suggesting—the motion of her thought process.

Motion in solo recital reflects at the gross level the nature of emotion, and more minutely the structure of thought. But, we must ask in conclusion, what is the scale in such imitation, to recall Lavane's distinction between operatic and recital gesture, or its level of realism, to draw on Hoffman's reliance on exercises from the naturalistic drama?

Marie Jean Guyau asserted the supreme significance of observable energy states over overt gesture and declared that although we may empathize with the body and limbs executing a movement,

> we empathize still more with the will which moves the body and limbs; the energy of this will may seduce us even more than the easy play of the members; and the ends it seeks be more attractive than a movement without a goal; finally, there comes a moment when one almost totally discounts the limbs which are reduced to the role of instruments, tense and bent like a bow ready to release an arrow, sometimes even spent by their effort (in Souriau 1983, 104).

The bulk of Lotte Lehmann's book More Than Singing: The Interpretation of Songs is given over to musical and dramatic suggestions for the performance of 86 songs, most of them Lieder. Her inspirational introduction to the book is perhaps its best known section. Aksel Schiøtz both referred to and commended it in his recital manual. In both the introduction and in her treatment of the performance of individual songs, Lehmann stressed the role of the imagination in creating the proper atmosphere for each song. Her strategy is in a sense the song recitalist's equivalent of the Stanislavskian "as if," a condition in which the performer places himself in the position of the character and asks how he would respond if he were in such a situation:

> The fundamental basis of my conception is this: never approach a *Lied* just as a melody. Search for the ideas and feelings which underlie it and which will follow it. Out of what mood or situation was the poem born? What drama, what dream, what experience was the inspiration for its conception? I never begin to study a *Lied* without first considering what brought it to life. I must picture it so vividly that I feel it is my own soul, my own being, which is now creating it. . . .
>
> Not every young singer has the gift of imagination. All that is possible should be done to develop this capacity. Periods should be arranged in the daily plan of study which should be devoted entirely to developing imagination and expressing what is imagined. . . . For example: [students] should take a book and try to act as they would feel if they were happy and were about to read a gay romance, as if they were absent minded, or sad, or as if it is a forbidden book. . . . If they can learn to observe themselves in this training, learning to feel how an emotion can be expressed without either word or song, it may perhaps be easier to transfer this new ability to their singing (Lehmann 1985, 12–13).

For Lehmann as for Hoffman, the singer's ability to imagine the dramatic situation while singing—rather than to literally act it out—is the preferable solution. One performs the emotions and thought process depicted in song, but on a physical scale which indicates only that one can *imagine* the dramatic situation.

The "as if" mode peppers Lehmann's instructions for performing Schubert's "Gretchen am Spinnrade" ("Gretchen at the Spinning Wheel"): The singer is to "imagine that you are sitting beside a spinning wheel which turns ceaselessly under your nervous feet." She is instructed that "after 'sein Kuss' [his kiss] you fall back exhausted. (I mean, of course, only in your imagination.)" Further, she is to "Imagine that your head falls forward, your body exhausted and trembling is bent over the spinning wheel which continues with its monotonous melody as your feet go on turning it mechanically." And she must "sing the last 'Mein Ruh' ist hin' [my peace is gone] as if through tears." All the gestures which Lehmann recommends are merely visualized. Although it is impossible to execute them full out in the recital setting, their image will ineffably infuse the singer's performance with the evocative sense of emotional reality.

Above all, it is the singer's ability to imagine not just emotional response but *physical* response that will produce the appropriate effect in recital:

> Raise your head and look up as you sing: "Wo ich ihn nicht hab'" [Unless I can have him]. Your body should sway backward slightly so that there is a possibility of coming forward at—"mein armer Kopf" [my poor head]. *Imagine* that your hands grip your forehead with the palms pressed against your temples. If you can make this gesture real in your thoughts you will have the right expression (Lehmann 1985, 22).

It is the *trace* of gesture, the evidence of the singer's desire to perform physically, to render emotion through the body, that is perhaps the keynote of the kinesthetic character of song performance. The reduction, abstraction, or distillation of the physical expression of emotion into a *sign* of such expression thus bears witness to the singer's competence in the conventions of classical song performance, and shows that the physical performance of song involves subtle interplay between physical and mental responses—not only to the music, but to each other.

Performance of Popular Song: Elements of Contrast with Classical Style

What is specifically *classical* about art song performance? It is notable how the distinctions Edward Cone makes among the characters "portrayed" by the singer, by the accompanist's part, and by the "complete musical persona" become less relevant when applied to popular song than when used to understand the performance of art song. A look at the performance style of solo singers of popular music may help us to illuminate the physical traditions of the classical recital stage, as well as the conventions regulating the singer's relationship to his song. The examples below do not by any means, of course, exhaust style in all popular singing, but merely give points of contrast with the vastly more uniform style in art song.

Two videotapes of *The Judy Garland Show* (1963, 1964) reveal how the architecture and staging of the performance subtly influence our relationship to the performer. Garland first enters the stage from up-center and crosses down toward the audience, into a flood of applause—unlike the classical recitalist, who because of stage geography must enter either from the back of the audience (when, for example, performing in a church) or laterally from doors at the side of the stage (when performing on a traditional university or professional hall stage). Thus, while Garland has only to unite with the applause that welcomes her, the traditional recitalist can only begin to establish a direct, frontal relationship with the audience once she has reached the center of the stage. The recitalist's stage persona is never protected or embraced as such. According to recital manuals and conservatory training methods, the only public persona she can establish must be a friendly, grateful, eminently accessible version of herself. Aksel Schiøtz advised beginning recitalists on the accepted protocol:

> The dimming of the hall lights is your cue to enter. Your attitude should be one of happiness and gratification that so many people want to hear you perform. Through all the recital, but especially at your first entrance, it is essential to the success of your performance that you appear natural and genuine in your demeanour. Do not run onto the stage. Walk with dignity, even if the piano seems miles away (Schiøtz 1970, 175).

On one of her variety shows, Garland enters from behind a series of enormous rectangular blocks with great blown-up childhood pictures of her daughter, Liza Minnelli, on the front. Well miked, she turns upstage and sings to them. These blocks are the material representation of "Garland's" memories. Their presence frees her both from the mime's task to create through bodily sculpture a "positive area in the negative expanse of space" and from the recitalist's office to show in her face and subtle bodily gestures what she sees in her world and the response it evokes in her (Davis 1962, 62).

One learns from these videotapes just how liberating the use of a set can be for a solo singer. Because the visual and internal worlds of the song are both provided for her, Garland's responsibility to the audience rests overwhelmingly on clear aural communication—i.e., just the singing, without any imperative to convey through gestural means the meaning, intent, or emotional resonance of the song. The vocal styles of Garland and of Lena Horne, who is her guest on one of the shows, belie this independence of the popular singer's visual style from the content of a song. If one were to turn the sound off on the videotape, it would be difficult to guess accurately the subject or emotional tone of the two singers' music. When Garland depicts any emotion at all, it is depersonalized, emotion she watches someone else process rather than feels herself. In "As Long As He Needs Me" from the Broadway musical *Oliver!*, for example, it is difficult for us to believe that Garland is the person out of whom the experience of the song comes.

Garland plays jazzily with "inappropriate" affects. She darts in and out of singing "The Man That Got Away" as if it were the expression of her own emotion. Her head movements are easy, jaunty, and she smiles as if at a train of inner thoughts totally unrelated to the course of the song. A couple of phrases later, she performs the song for a moment with intense betrayed emotion. It is these facile transitions, this emotional lability, that fascinates us and makes us wonder to what degree we are supposed to believe in Garland as the protagonist of the song.

What would be abhorred in art song performance, Garland's arm movements are angular, sudden, and from the elbows, partly perhaps because she's got on the tight, rather awkward three-quarters length sleeves of the period, but also perhaps because what she is primarily communicating to the audience is her own full public personality *as a singer*, rather than her status as an empty vessel for inhabitation by twenty or so different characters over the span of an hour.

Horne takes this self-advancing stand toward her material a further swaggering step by creating tremendous contrasts among the energy styles of different parts of her body. Despite the nurturing content of her lyrics, "I want to be happy, but I'll never be happy, till I make you happy too," Horne sings them with riveting self-containment and self-stimulation. Her eyes, though, flash with fingers of fire. She juts her head side to side like an Indian dancer. She seductively shows us by the way she mouths the words the soft inner parts of her instrument. Her eyes roll and pop. In another song, Horne growls out in a lively conga rhythm, "Oh, I'm tinglin' such delicious tingles . . ." as a pouty, questionably pre-pubescent little West Indian kid. With a kind of drugged aspect, Horne perpetuates while she sings a private affair with the *way* she chooses to sing.

In part, the odd disjuncture between the lyrical content of these popular songs and singer's emotional detachment in performance is due to the characteristic style of setting lyrics in mid-twentieth century American popular music. The style paints energy, enthusiasm, and charisma for the performer more than it represents a character's private landscape. To a large extent, then, in the American style of popular music performance the singer responds externally, as a dancer, rather than internally, as a thinker, to the accompaniment, thus dissolving the concept of the "instrumental persona" which Cone ascribes to the accompaniment in song and of which he says that the singer is often unconscious. During introductions, interludes, and postludes to songs, Garland and Horne both dance with the music, even covering some fair stage space. With an onstage orchestra, Judy Collins turns sideways towards it and prances laterally facing the players, as if to indicate her visceral enjoyment of her colleagues' work. Even at the level of vocalism, these popular singers are in no private world, unconscious of the fact that their expressions are stylized (like Hamlet speaking English blank verse instead of Danish prose). When Garland's background singers drop in for her "As Long As He Needs Me," she stops suddenly as if to listen for a moment and smiles to herself, as if at their fine harmony.

Physically, Edith Piaf's concerts share stylistic aspects both with recital performance and with the popular singing of Garland, Horne, and Collins. Piaf performs "as if" the emotional content of the songs were a reflection of her own emotional life. As an audience, we of course cannot help but be affected by our knowledge that they share an intimate connection with Piaf's troubled private life. In addition, the fact that Piaf's songs have been, many of them, penned by their singer proves an inescapable bond between the singer's life and her material. In a videotaped interview as part of a memorial to the beloved French singer, one of Piaf's colleagues said of her that she was always "looking for a new way to die" through song. Piaf's gestures have emotional resonance, as she presses her hands to her breast, her chin, and her face while she sings. Even though gesturing this high on the body is generally discouraged in recitalists (Antonia Lavane, in chapter 2, found this style too "operatic"), similar gestures are often performed in recital lower on or farther from the body, though often without evidence of the singer's being so greatly affected by the emotion of the work. At the same time, the nearness of Piaf's hands to her upper torso and face closely resembles the way Judy Collins handles a microphone in concert, which necessitates her keeping the instrument—and thus also her hands—close to her body, between her mouth and upper torso.

Microphone technique in concert raises an essential point about visual focus for popular singers. Judy Collins' visual focus seems geared neither to creating visually a world that she "sees" in front of her nor to drawing the audience in. Rather, she closes her eyes perhaps 20 to 30% of the time as she sings, then keeps track of where the microphone cord has travelled, as well as other logistical matters, without an evident break in mood or objective. The process of visual focus is divorced from the process of communicating the meaning of a song, and she seems to expect that the audience will understand the song without specific visual cues from her. She even makes a generalized kind of "picturing" gesture, drawing her flat hand across the plane facing her directly in front, as if to say (with no greater specificity), "Just see it."

Collins' between-song patter and the variety-show chitchat of Garland and Horne seem to distance the audience more from the performer than does the performance of the actual music. The formal, rehearsed quality of Collins' and Garland's obviously oft-repeated comments separates us from the singers and makes us feel that we know them less well in these moments than when they sing, even though Allen held that two of the purposes of transitional remarks by the solo performer are "to reveal or indicate something about the creative process of the interpreter who chooses the material and orders the presentation . . . [and to] reveal the performer's attitude toward his role as performer and toward the material itself" (Allen 1984, 251). In recital performance, any of the rare remarks a singer makes between groups of songs or before encores indeed reveals such aspects of the singer's artistry; one senses in recital performance that one gets to know the singer better as a person and as an artist by these informal comments.

Thus, popular song performance departs in certain significant ways from that of classical song, among them the performer's ability to use stage space, costume, scenery, and props; the relationship among the musical, lexical, and emotional signs that are delivered to the audience; the persona of the performer; and the implicit relationship between the singer and the song.

Bibliography

PRINTED MATERIALS

Allen, John J.
1984   "Physical and Oral Behaviors of the Solo Oral Interpretive Performer: A Classification and Synthesis of Current Theory, With Advice for Practical Application." Unpublished Ph.D. dissertation, Wayne State University.

Austin, Gilbert
1966   *Chironomia, or a Treatise on Rhetorical Delivery*. Mary Margaret Robb and Lestern Thonnsen, eds. Carbondale and Edwardsville: Southern Illinois University Press.

Balk, Wesley
1985   *Performing Power: A New Approach for the Singer-Actor*. Minneapolis: University of Minnesota Press.
1977   *The Complete Singer-Actor: Training for Music Theater*. Minneapolis: University of Minnesota Press.

Barnett, Dene
1980–81 "The Performance Practice of Acting: The Eighteenth Century. Part V: Posture and Attitudes." *Theatre Research International*. Winter. 6(1):1–32.
1980   "Finding the Appropriate Attitude." *Early Music*. Interviewed by Ian Parker. January. 8(1):65–69.
1979–80 "The Performance Practice of Acting: The Eighteenth Century. Part IV: The Eyes, the Face and the Head." *Theatre Research International*. Winter. 5(1):1–36.
1977   "The Performance Practice of Acting: The Eighteenth Century. Part II: The Hands." *Theatre Research International*. October. 3(1):1–29.

Barnett, Dene (continued),
1976   "The Performance Practice of Acting: The Eighteenth Century. Part I: Ensemble Acting." *Theatre Research International.* 2(3):157–87.

Barrault, Jean-Louis
1961   "The Tragic Mime." In *The Mime.* Jean Dorcy, ed., pp. 89–100. New York: Robert Speller and Sons.

Bernac, Pierre
1970   *The Interpretation of French Song.* New York: W. W. Norton.

Blacking, John
1977   *The Anthropology of the Body.* London: Academic Press.

Caruso, Enrico and Tetrazzini, Luisa
1975   *Caruso and Tetrazzini on the Art of Singing.* New York: Dover Publications, Inc.

Cone, Edward T.
1974   *The Composer's Voice.* Berkeley: University of California Press.

Davis, R. G.
1962   "Method in Mime." The Drama Review. 6(4). T-16. (Summer 1962), pp. 61–65.

Decroux, Etienne
1961   "For Better and For Worse." In *The Mime.* Jean Dorcy, ed., pp. 77–87. New York: Robert Speller and Sons.

Dorcy, Jean, ed.
1961   *The Mime.* New York: Robert Speller and Sons.

Dorian, Frederick
1942   *The History of Music in Performance: The Art of Musical Interpretation From the Renaissance to Our Day.* New York: W. W. Norton and Co.

Dowland, John
1979   "Andreas Ornithoparcus his Micrologus (1609)." In *Readings in the History of Music in Performance.* Carol MacClintock, ed. Bloomington: Indiana University Press.

Ekman, Paul
1977   "Biological and Cultural Contributions to Body and Facial Movement." In *Anthropology of the Body.* John Blacking, ed., pp. 39–84. London: Academic Press.

Emmons, Shirlee and Sonntag, Stanley
1979   *The Art of the Song Recital.* New York: Schirmer Books.

Gentile, John Samuel
1984   "The One-Person Show in America: From the Victorian Platform to the Contemporary Stage." Unpublished Ph.D. dissertation, Northwestern University.

Goldstein, Malcolm
1985   "Notes on the Gesture of Sound." *Contact Quarterly.* 10(1):42–43. Winter.

Greene, Harry Plunket
1979   *Interpretation in Song.* New York: Da Capo Press.

Guilbert, Yvette
1918   *How to Sing a Song.* New York: Macmillan.

Holmstrom, Kirsten Gram
1967   *Monodrama, Attitudes, Tableaux Vivants: Studies on Some Trends in Theatrical Fashion, 1770–1815.* Stockholm: Almqvist and Wiksell.

Lehmann, Lotte
1985   *More Than Singing: The Interpretation of Songs.* Frances Holden, trans. New York: Dover Publications.

Leyerle, William D.
1977   *Vocal Development Through Organic Imagery.* New York: Geneseo.

Long, Chester Clayton
1974   *The Liberal Art of Interpretation.* New York: Harper and Row.

Marceau, Marcel
1961   "The Poetic Halo." In *The Mime.* Jean Dorcy, ed., pp. 101–5. New York: Robert Speller and Sons.

Martens, Frederick H.
1923   *The Art of the Prima Donna and Concert Singer.* New York: D. Appleton and Co.

Massy-Westropp, Jeanette
1984   "Idealization of Characters and Specialization of Acting in Eighteenth-Century Tragedy: The Villain." *Theatre Research International.* Summer. 9(2):111–27.

Monahan, Brent Jeffrey
1978   *The Art of Singing: A Compendium of Thoughts on Singing Published Between 1777 and 1927.* Methuchen, NJ: The Scarecrow Press.

Morgan, Anna
1889   *An Hour With Delsarte: A Study of Expression.* Boston: Lee and Shepard Publishers.

Plax, Pamela Miller
1976   "Guidelines for Interpretive Performance of Four Narrative Genres: Commentator, Dramatized Narrator, Scenic Narration, and Internal Narration". Unpublished Ph.D. dissertation, University of Southern California.

Praetorius, Michael
1979   "Syntagma Musicum." In *Readings in the History of Music in Performance.* Carol MacClintock, ed. Bloomington: Indiana University Press.

Raynor, Henry
1972   *A Social History of Music: From the Middle Ages to Beethoven.* London: Barrie and Jenkins.

Schiøtz, Aksel
1970   *The Singer and His Art.* New York: Harper and Row.

Shawn, Ted
1954   *Every Little Movement.* New York: M. Witmark and Sons.

Souriau, Paul
1983   *The Aesthetics of Movement.* Manon Souriau, trans. University of Massachusetts Press.

Stebbins, Genevieve
1977   *The Delsarte System of Expression.* New York: Dance Horizons.

Warman, Edward B.
1892   *Gestures and Attitudes: An Exposition of the Delsarte Philosophy of Expression, Practical and Theoretical.* Boston: Lee and Shepard Publishers.

Winn, James Anderson
1981   *Unsuspected Eloquence: A History of the Relations Between Poetry and Music.* New Haven: Yale University Press.

Young, Percy M.
1965   *The Concert Tradition: From the Middle Ages to the Twentieth Century.*
          London: Routledge and Kegan Paul.

CLASSES, LECTURES

Everding, August. Lecture on the boundary between music theatre and opera, Aspen Music Festival, Aspen, Colorado, August 7, 1988.

Hoffman, Cynthia. Class in Vocal Performance, Manhattan School of Music, New York, New York, January 25, 1988.

Lavane, Antonia. Class in Song Interpretation, Mannes College of Music, New York, New York, January 21, 1988.

Scimone, Claudio. Lecture on Rossini, Aspen Music Festival, Aspen, Colorado, July 24, 1987.

Sperry, Paul. Classes in Song Repertoire, the Aspen Music 73 Festival, Aspen, Colorado, June–August, 1987. Classes in American Song and in 20th Century Song, the Juilliard School, New York, New York, January 18, 22, 25, 1988.

VIDEOTAPES

Aldeburgh Master Classes: The Britten-Pears School for Advanced Musical Research, No. 1.

Callas, Maria. "Maria Callas in Concert." At Hamburg Music Hall, Hamburg, Germany. 5/15/59. 60 minutes.

Collins, Judy. "This is the Day." Judy Collins in concert with the Hamilton Place Symphony Orchestra. 120 minutes.

Crespin, Regine. Master class at Mannes College, 11/7/87.

Galupe-Borszkh, Vera (Ira Siff). Second Annual Farewell Recitals. With Maestro Francesco Folinari-Soave-Coglioni (Ross Barentyne) at the piano. La Gran Scena Opera Company at Don't Tell Mama, New York, New York, October 18, 1987.

Garland, Judy. "The Judy Garland Show." 2 videotapes of televised variety show with guest stars Liza Minnelli and Lena Horne. 1963 and 1964.

Kelly, John. "All About Art: A Retrospective of Early Work by John Kelly." Presented by Dance Chance. Taped 4/15/87 at St. Mark's Church.

Kelly, John. "The Discovery of Sound (Born With The Moon in Cancer)." Taped at Tweed Third Annual New Works Festival, New York, New York, Thursday, May 22, 1986.

Ludwig, Christa. "A Brahms Lieder Recital." Recorded at Tel Aviv Museum. WNET/TV-13 Great Performances; air date 6/13/78. Producer: David Griffiths. 60 minutes.

Piaf, Edith. "I Regret Nothing." A Musical Biography by Michael Houldey. BBC documentary. 1979. 90 minutes.

Schwarzkopf, Elisabeth. "Elisabeth Schwarzkopf Master Class." Taped, narrated excerpts from series of master classes held at the Edinburgh Festival. 1980. 45 minutes.

Wunderlich, Fritz. "Portraet eines Saengers." Written and directed by Manfred Deide. 30 minutes.

INTERVIEWS

Kelly, John. New York, New York, February 22, 1988.

Sperry, Paul. New York, New York, February 3, 1988.

LIVE PERFORMANCES

Galupe-Borszkh, Vera (Ira Siff). Second Annual Farewell Recitals. With Maestro Francesco Folinari-Soave-Coglioni (Ross Barentyne) at the piano. La Gran Scena Opera Company at Don't Tell Mama, New York, New York, Sunday, November 6, 1987 at 5:00 p.m.

Kelly, John. "The Discovery of Sound (Born With the Moon in Cancer)." Performed at the Tweed Third Annual New Works Festival, New York, New York, Thursday, May 22, 1986 and in Aspen, Colorado, Sunday, July 11, 1987 at 7:00 p.m.

Liederabend, the Juilliard School, Paul Hall, New York, New York, Tuesday, February 2, 1988 at 6:00 p.m. Recital of art songs in English by non-native singers at the School.

Prey, Herman. Master class at Manhattan School of Music, New York, New York, Thursday, October 15, 1987 at 7:00 p.m.

Singers' auditions for Opera Theater Center, Aspen Music Festival, Aspen, Colorado, June 23–24, 1987.